ISBN 978-1-331-42217-4
PIBN 10187948

FB &c Ltd, Dalton House, 60 Windsor Avenue, London, SW19 2RR.
Company number 08720141. Registered in England and Wales.

PREFACE.

On the 5th March, 1872, in moving that the "Indian "Evidence Act" should be taken into consideration by the Legislative Council, I said—"many topics "closely connected with the subject of Evidence are "incapable of being satisfactorily dealt with by ex-"press law. It would be easy to dilate upon the theory "on which the whole subject rests, and the manner in "which an Act of this kind should be used in practice. "I think, however, that it would not be proper to "do so on the present occasion. I have therefore "put into writing what I have to say on these "subjects, and I propose to publish what I have "written, by way of a commentary upon, or intro-"duction to, the Act itself. I hope that this may be "some use to Civil Servants who are preparing "in England for their Indian career, and to the law "students in Indian universities. The subject is "one which reaches far beyond law. The law of "evidence is nothing unless it is founded upon a "rational conception of the manner in which truth "as to all matters of fact whatever ought to be in-"vestigated."

This, written for the most part before these remarks were made, but corrected and completed since my return to England, is the Introduction referred to.

August 30*th*, 1872.

4, Paper Buildings, Temple.

*

POSTSCRIPT.

In the *Gazette of India* of August 17, 1872, a Bill for the Amendment of the Evidence Act is published for the first time. In the Statement of Objects and Reasons appended to the Bill it is said that "the primary object of this Bill is to continue certain rules which it is believed were inadvertently repealed by the Indian Evidence Act." It is added that "at the same time opportunity is taken to correct some clerical and other accidental errors to which attention has been called."

If the Bill has already become or should hereafter become law in its present shape, the following *errata* should be made in the Act as printed below :—

1. S. 32, clauses 5 and 6, after "relationship" insert "by blood, marriage, or adoption."
2. S. 41, in each of the last three paragraphs, after the word "judgment" add the words "order or decree."
3. S. 45, after the word "art" add "or in questions as to the identity of handwriting."
4. S. 57, paragraph 13, after the word "road" add "on land or at sea."
5. S. 66, after "in whose possession the document is" add "or to his attorney or pleader."

6. In S. 91, exception (2), for "under the Indian Succession Act" read "admitted to probate in British India."
7. In S. 92, proviso 1, for "want of failure" read "want or failure."
8. In S. 108, for "when" read "provided that when," and for the word "on" in the last line read "shifted to."
9. In S. 126 (paragraph immediately preceding the explanation) and in section 128 insert "pleader" after "barrister."
10. In S. 126 paragraph 2, for "criminal" read "illegal."
11. In S. 155, paragraph 2, for "or has had the offer of a bribe" read "or has accepted the offer of a bribe."
12. In the repealing schedule No. 3, third column, add "except section 12."

Of these *errata* three, viz., Nos. 8, 10, and 11, make substantial alterations in the Act on points on which it was drawn advisedly in the words in which it now stands, for various reasons which were carefully considered and regarded as satisfactory. Upon these points there is of course room for difference of opinion, but there was no inadvertence.

September 30*th*, 1872.
4, Paper Buildings, Temple.

TABLE OF CONTENTS OF INTRODUCTION.

CHAPTER I.

GENERAL DISTRIBUTION OF THE SUBJECT.—Pp. 1—12.

CHAPTER II.

A STATEMENT OF THE PRINCIPLES OF INDUCTION AND DEDUCTION, AND A COMPARISON OF THEIR APPLICATION TO SCIENTIFIC AND JUDICIAL INQUIRIES—Pp. 13—15.

CHAPTER III.

THE THEORY OF RELEVANCY, WITH ILLUSTRATION.

Pp. 52—128.

CHAPTER IV.

GENERAL OBSERVATIONS ON THE INDIAN EVIDENCE ACT.—Pp. 129—134.

THE

PRINCIPLES OF JUDICIAL EVIDENCE

BEING AN INTRODUCTION TO THE

INDIAN EVIDENCE ACT

(I. of 1872).

CHAPTER I.

GENERAL DISTRIBUTION OF THE SUBJECT.

CHAP. I.

Technical and general elements of law.

Almost every branch of law is composed of rules of which some are grounded upon practical convenience and the experience of actual litigation, whilst others are closely connected with the constitution of human nature and society. Thus the criminal law contains many provisions of no general interest, such as those which relate to the various forms in which dishonest persons tamper with or imitate coin; but it also contains provisions, such as those which relate to the effect of madness on responsibility, which depend on several of the most interesting branches of moral and physical learning. This is perhaps more conspicuously true of the law of evidence than of any other branch of the law. Many of its provisions, however useful and necessary, are technical; and the enactments in which they are contained can claim no other merit than those of completeness and perspicuity. The whole subject of documentary evidence is of this nature. Other branches of the subject, such as the relevancy of facts, are intimately connected with the whole theory of human knowledge, and with logic, as applied to human conduct. The object of this introduction is to illustrate these parts of the subject, by stating the theory on which they depend and on which the provisions of the Act proceed. As to more

CHAP. I. technical matters, the Act speaks for itself, and I have nothing to add to its contents.

Relation of Evidence Act to English law of evidence.

The Indian Evidence Act is little more than an attempt to reduce the English law of evidence to the form of express propositions arranged in their natural order, with some modifications rendered necessary by the peculiar circumstances of India.

English law of evidence.

Like almost every other part of English law, the English law of evidence was formed by degrees. No part of the law has been left so entirely to the discretion of successive generations of Judges. The Legislature till very recently interfered but little with the matter, and since it began to interfere, it has done so principally by repealing particular rules, such as that which related to the disqualification of witnesses by interest, and that which excluded the testimony of the parties; but it has not attempted to deal with the main principles of the subject.

Its want of arrangement.

It is natural that a body of law thus formed by degrees, and with reference to particular cases, should be destitute of arrangement, and in particular that its leading terms should never have been defined by authority; that general rules should have been laid down with reference rather to particular circumstances than to general principles, and that it should have been found necessary to qualify them by exceptions inconsistent with the principles on which they proceed.

Difficulties of amending it.

When this confusion had once been introduced into the subject it was hardly capable of being remedied either by courts of law, or by writers of text-books. The courts of law could only decide the cases which came before them according to the rules in force. The writers of text-books could only collect the results of such decisions. The Legislature might, no doubt, have remedied the evil, but comprehensive legislation upon abstract questions of law has never yet been attempted by Parliament in any one instance, though it has in several well-known cases been attended with signal success in India.

That part of the English law of evidence which professes to be founded upon anything in the nature of a theory on the subject may be reduced to the following rules :—

CHAP. I.

Fundamental rules of English law of evidence.

(1) Evidence must be confined to the matters in issue.

(2) Hearsay evidence is not to be admitted.

(3) In all cases the best evidence must be given.

Each of these rules is very loosely expressed. The word 'evidence,' which is the leading term of each, is undefined and ambiguous.

It sometimes means the words uttered and things exhibited by witnesses before a court of justice.

At other times, it means the facts proved to exist by those words or things, and regarded as the groundwork of inferences as to other facts not so proved.

Again, it is sometimes used as meaning to assert that a particular fact is relevant to the matter under inquiry.

The word 'issue' is ambiguous. In many cases it is used with reference to the strict rules of English special pleading, the main object of which is to define, with great accuracy, the precise matter which is affirmed by the one party to a suit, and denied by the other.

In other cases it is used as embracing generally the whole subject under inquiry.

Again, the word 'hearsay' is used in various senses. Sometimes it means whatever a person is heard to say; sometimes it means whatever a person declares on information given by some one else; sometimes it is treated as being nearly synonymous with 'irrelevant.'

Ambiguity of rule as to confining evidence to issue.

If the rule that evidence must be confined to the matters in issue were construed strictly, it would run thus: 'No witness shall ever depose to any fact, except those facts which by the form of the pleadings are affirmed on the one side and denied on the other.' So understood, the rule would obviously put a stop to the whole administration of justice, as it would exclude evidence of decisive facts.

A sues B on a promissory note. B denies that he made the note.

A has a letter from B in which he admits that he made the note, and promises to pay it. This admission could not be proved if the rule referred to were construed strictly, because the issue is, whether B made the note, and not whether he admitted having made it.

This absurd result is avoided by using the word 'evidence' as meaning not testimony but any fact from which any other fact may be inferred. Thus interpreted, the rule that evidence, must be confined to matters in issue will run thus: 'No facts may be proved to exist, except facts in issue or facts from which the existence of the facts in issue can be inferred;' but if the rule is thus interpreted, it becomes so vague as to be of little use; for the question naturally arises, from what sort of facts may the existence of other facts be inferred? To this question the law of England gives no explicit answer at all, though partial and confused answers to parts of it may be inferred from some of the exceptions to the rule which excludes hearsay.

For instance, there are cases from which it may be inferred that evidence may sometimes be given of a fact from which another fact may be inferred, although the fact upon which the inference is to be founded is a crime, and although the fact to be inferred is also a crime for which the person against whom the evidence is to be given is on his trial.

The full answer to the question, 'what facts are relevant,' which is the most important of all the questions that can be asked about the law of evidence, has thus to be learnt partly by experience, and partly by collecting together such crooked and narrow illustrations of it as the one just given.

Ambiguity of the rule excluding hearsay.

The rule that 'hearsay is no evidence' is vague to the last degree, as each of the meanings of which the word 'hearsay' is susceptible is sometimes treated as the true one. As the rule is nowhere laid down in an authoritative manner, its meaning has to be collected from the exceptions to it, and these exceptions, of which there are as many as twelve or thirteen, imply at least three different meanings of the word 'hearsay.'

Thus it is a rule that evidence may be given of statements which accompany and explain relevant actions. As no rule determines what actions are relevant, this is in itself unsatisfactory; but as the rule is treated as an exception to the rule excluding hearsay, it implies that 'hearsay' means that which a man is heard to say. If this is the meaning of hearsay, the rule which excludes it would run thus: 'No witness shall ever be allowed to depose to any thing which he has heard said by any one else.' The result of this would be that no verbal contract could ever be proved, and that no one could ever be convicted of using threats with intent to extort money, or of defamation by words spoken, except in virtue of exceptions which stultify the rule.

Most of the exceptions indicate that the meaning of the word 'hearsay' is that which a person reports on the information of some one else, and not upon the evidence of his own senses. This, with certain exceptions, is no doubt a valuable rule, but it is not the natural meaning of the words 'hearsay is no evidence,' and it is in practice almost impossible to divest words of their natural meaning.

The rule that documents which support ancient possession may be admitted as between person who are not parties to them, is treated as an exception to the rule excluding hearsay. This implies that the word 'hearsay' is nearly, if not quite, equivalent to the word 'irrelevant.' But the English law contains nothing which approaches to a definition of relevancy.

Rules as to best evidence.

The rule which requires that the best evidence of which a fact is susceptible should be given, is the most distinct of the three rules referred to above, and it is certainly one of the most useful. It is simply an amplification of the obvious maxim, that if a man wishes to know all that he can know about a matter, his own senses are to him the highest possible authority. If a hundred witnesses of unimpeachable character were all to swear to the contents of a sealed letter, and if the person who heard them swear opened the letter

CHAP. I.

and found that its contents were different, he would conclude, without the intervention of any conscious process of reasoning at all, that they had sworn what was not true.

Ambiguity of the word 'evidence.'

The ambiguity of the word 'evidence' is the cause of a great deal of obscurity apart from that which it gives to the rules above mentioned. In scientific inquiries, and for popular and general purposes, it is no doubt convenient to have one word which includes—

(1) The testimony on which a given fact is believed.

(2) the facts so believed, and

(3) the arguments founded upon them.

For instance, in the title of "Paley's Evidences of Christianity," the word is used in this sense. The nature of the work was not such as to give much importance to the distinction which the word overlooks. So, in scientific inquiries, it is seldom necessary (for reasons to which I shall have occasion to refer hereafter) to lay stress upon the difference between the testimony on which a fact is believed, and the fact itself. In judicial inquiries, however, the distinction is most important, and the neglect to observe it has thrown the whole subject into confusion by causing English lawyers to overlook the leading distinction which ought to form the principle on which the whole law should be classified. I mean the distinction between the relevancy of facts and the mode of proving relevant facts.

Effects of this ambiguity.

The use of the one name 'evidence' for the fact to be proved, and the means by which it is to be proved, has given a double meaning to every phrase in which the word occurs. Thus, for instance, the phrase 'primary evidence' sometimes means a relevant fact, and sometimes the original of a document as opposed to a copy. 'Circumstantial evidence' is opposed to 'direct evidence.' But 'circumstantial evidence usually means a fact, from which some other fact is inferred, whereas 'direct evidence' means testimony given by a man as to what he has himself perceived by his own senses. It would thus be correct to say that circumstantial evidence must be proved by direct evidence—a clumsy mode of expression, which is in itself a mark of confusion of thought. The evil, however, goes beyond mere clumsiness of expression. People have naturally enough supposed that circumstantial and direct evidence admit of being contrasted in respect of their cogency, and that different canons can be laid down, as to the conditions which they ought to satisfy before the court is convinced by them. This, I think, confuses the theory of proof, and is an error, due entirely to the ambiguity of the word 'evidence.'

Merits of English law of evidence.

It would be a mistake to infer from the unsystematic character and absence of arrangement which belong to the English law of evidence that the substance of the law itself is bad. On the contrary, it possesses in the highest degree the characteristic merits of English case law. English case law, as it is, is to what it ought to be, and might be, if it were properly arranged, what the ordinary conversation of a very clever man on all sorts of subjects written down as he uttered it, and as passing circumstances furnished him with a text, would be to the matured and systematic statement of his deliberate opinions. It is full of the most vigorous sense, and is the result of great sagacity applied to vast and varied experience.

Natural distribution of the subject.

The manner in which the law of evidence is related to the general theories which give it its interest can be understood only by reference to the natural distribution of the subject, which appears to be as follows ;—

All rights and liabilities are dependent upon and arise out of facts.

Every judicial proceeding whatever has for its purpose the ascertaining of some right or liability. If the proceeding is criminal, the object is to ascertain the liability to punishment of the person accused. If the proceeding is civil, the object is to ascertain some right of property or of status, or the right of one party, and the liability of the other, to some form of relief.

CHAP. I.

In order to effect this result, provision must be made by law for the following objects:—*First,* the legal effect of particular classes of facts in establishing rights and liabilities must be determined. This is the province of what has been called substantive law. *Secondly,* a course of procedure must be laid down by which persons interested may apply the substantive law to particular cases.

The law of procedure includes, amongst others, two main branches,—(1) the law of pleading, which determines what in particular cases are the questions in dispute between the parties, and (2) the law of evidence, which determines how the parties are to convince the court of the existence of that state of facts which, according to the provisions of substantive law, would establish the existence of the right or liability which they allege to exist.

Illustration.

The following is a simple illustration: A sues B on a bond for Rs. 1,000. B says that the execution of the bond was procured by coercion.

The substantive law is, that a bond executed under coercion cannot be enforced.

The law of procedure lays down the method according to which A is to establish his right to the payment of the sum secured by the bond. One of its provisions determines the manner in which the question between the parties is to be stated.

The question stated under that provision is, whether the execution of the bond was procured by coercion.

The law of evidence determines—

(1) What sort of facts may be proved in order to establish the existence of that which is defined by the substantive law as coercion.

(2) What sort of proof is to be given of those facts.

(3) Who is to give it.

(4) How is it to be given.

Thus, before the law of evidence can be understood or applied to any particular case, it is necessary to know so much of the substantive law as determines what, under given states of fact, would be the rights of the parties, and so much of the law of procedure as is sufficient to determine what questions it is open to them to raise in the particular proceeding. CHAP. I.

Thus in general terms the law of evidence consists of provisions upon the following subjects : Result.

(1) The relevancy of facts.

(2) The proof of facts.

(3) The production of proof of relevant facts.

The foregoing observations show that this account of the matter is exhaustive. For if we assume that a fact is known to be relevant, and that its existence is duly proved, the Court is in a position to go on to say how it affects the existence, nature, or extent of the right or liability, the ascertainment of which is the ultimate object of the inquiry, and this is all that the Court has to do.

The matter must, however, be carried further. The three general heads may be distributed more particularly as follows ·

I .*The Relevancy of Facts.*—Facts may be related to rights and liabilities in one of two ways,— Relevancy of facts. 1 Facts in issue.

(1) They may by themselves, or in connection with other facts, constitute such a state of things that the existence of the disputed right or liability would be a legal inference from them. From the fact that A is the eldest son of B, there arises of necessity the inference that A is by the law of England the heir-at-law of B, and that he has such rights as that status involves. From the fact that A caused the death of B under certain circumstances, and with a certain intention or knowledge, there arises of necessity the inference that A murdered B, and is liable to the punishment provided by law for murder.

Facts thus related to a proceeding may be called facts in issue, unless their existence is undisputed.

(2) Facts, which are not themselves in issue in the sense above explained, may affect the probability of the existence 2. Relevant facts.

CHAP. I. of facts in issue, and be used as the foundation of inferences respecting them; such facts are described in the Evidence Act as relevant facts.

All the facts with which it can in any event be necessary for courts of justice to concern themselves, are included in these two classes.

The first great question, therefore, which the law of evidence should decide is, what facts are relevant. The answer to this question is to be learnt from the general theory of judicial evidence explained in the following chapter.

What facts are in issue in particular cases is a question to be determined by the substantive law, or in some instances by that branch of the law of procedure which regulates the forms of pleading, civil or criminal.

Proof of relevant facts.

II. *The Proof of Relevant Facts.*—Whether an alleged fact is a fact in issue or a relevant fact, the court can draw no inference from its existence till it believes it to exist; and it is obvious that the belief of the court in the existence of a given fact ought to proceed upon grounds altogether independent of the relation of the fact to the object and nature of the proceeding in which its existence is to be determined. The question is whether A wrote a letter. The letter may have contained the terms of a contract. It may have been a libel. It may have constituted the motive for the commission of a crime by B. It may supply proof of an *alibi* in favour of A. It may be an admission or a confession of crime; but whatever may be the relation of the fact to the proceeding, the court cannot act upon it unless it believes that A did write the letter, and that belief must obviously be produced, in each of the cases mentioned, by the same or similar means. If the court requires the production of the original when the writing of the letter is a crime, there can be no reason why it should be satisfied with a copy when the writing of the letter is a motive for a crime. In short, the way in which a fact should be proved depends on the nature of the fact, and not on the relation of the fact to the proceeding.

1. Judicia notice. 2. Oral evidence. 3. Documentary evidence.

Some facts are too notorious to require any proof at all, and of these the court will take judicial notice; but if a fact does require proof, the instrument by which the court must be convinced of it is evidence; by which I mean the actual words uttered, or documents, or other things actually produced in court, and not the facts which the court considers to be proved by those words and documents. Evidence in this sense of the word must be either (1) oral or (2) documentary. A third class might be formed of things produced in court, not being documents, such as the instruments with which a crime was committed, or the property to which damage had been done, but this division would introduce needless intricacy into the matter. The reason for distinguising between oral and documentary evidence is that in many cases the existence of the latter excludes the employment of the former; but the condition of material things, other than documents, is usually proved by oral evidence, so that there is no occasion to distinguish between oral and material evidence.

It may be said that in strictness all evidence is oral, as documents or other material things must be identified by oral evidence before the court can take notice of them. It is unnecessary to discuss the justice of this criticism, as the phrase 'documentary evidence' is not ambiguous, and is convenient and in common use. The only reason for avoiding the use of the word 'evidence' in the general sense in which most writers use it, is that it leads, in practice, to confusion, as has been already pointed out.

Production of proof.

III. *The Production of Proof.*—This includes the subject of the burden of proof: the rules upon which answer the question, By whom is proof to be given? The subject of witnesses: the rules upon which answer the question, who is to give evidence, and under what conditions? The subject of the examination of witnesses: the rules upon which answer the question, How are the witnesses to be examined, and how is their evidence to be tested? Lastly, the effect upon

CHAP. I. the subsequent proceedings, of mistakes in the reception and rejection of evidence may be included under this head.

The following tabular scheme of the subject may be an assistance to the reader. The figures refer to the sections of the Act which treat of the matter referred to :—

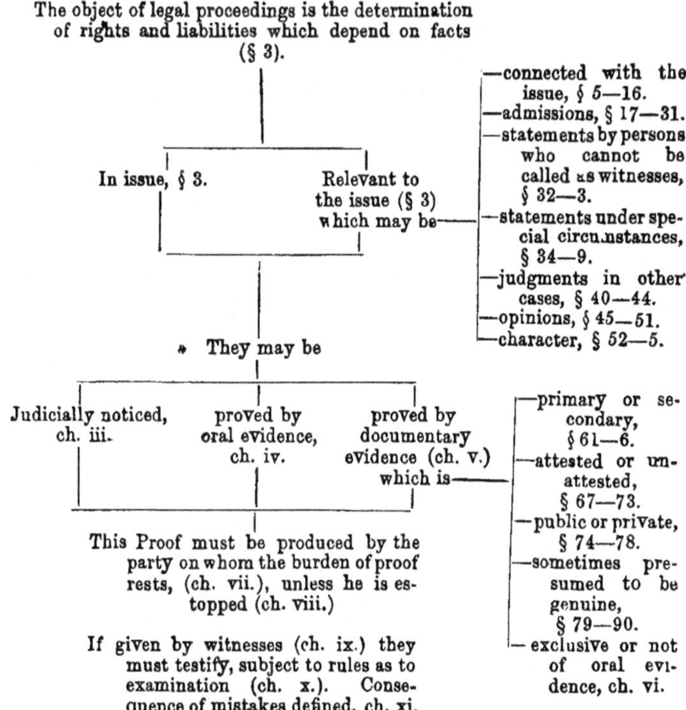
The object of legal proceedings is the determination of rights and liabilities which depend on facts (§ 3).
In issue, § 3.
Relevant to the issue (§ 3) which may be
—connected with the issue, § 5—16.
—admissions, § 17—31.
—statements by persons who cannot be called as witnesses, § 32—3.
—statements under special circumstances, § 34—9.
—judgments in other cases, § 40—44.
—opinions, § 45—51.
—character, § 52—5.
They may be
Judicially noticed, ch. iii.
proved by oral evidence, ch. iv.
proved by documentary evidence (ch. v.) which is
—primary or secondary, § 61—6.
—attested or unattested, § 67—73.
—public or private, § 74—78.
—sometimes presumed to be genuine, § 79—90.
—exclusive or not of oral evidence, ch. vi.
This Proof must be produced by the party on whom the burden of proof rests, (ch. vii.), unless he is estopped (ch. viii.)
If given by witnesses (ch. ix.) they must testify, subject to rules as to examination (ch. x.). Consequence of mistakes defined, ch. xi.

CHAPTER II.

A STATEMENT OF THE PRINCIPLES OF INDUCTION AND DEDUCTION, AND A COMPARISON OF THEIR APPLICATION TO SCIENTIFIC AND JUDICIAL INQUIRIES.

CHAP. II.

THE general analysis given in the last chapter of the subjects to which the law of evidence must relate, sufficiently explains the general arrangement of the Indian Evidence Act. To understand the substance of the Act it is necessary to have some acquaintance with the general theory of judicial evidence. The object of the present chapter is to explain this theory and to compare its application to physical science with its application to judicial inquiries.

Mr. Huxley on physical science and judicial inquiries.

Mr. Huxley remarks in one of his latest works—"The vast results obtained by science are won by no mystical faculties, by no mental processes, other than those which are practised by every one of us in the humblest and meanest affairs of life. A detective policeman discovers a burglar from the marks made by his shoe, by a mental process identical with that by which Cuvier restored the extinct animals of Montmartre from fragments of their bones, nor does that process of induction and deduction by which a lady finding a stain of a particular kind upon her dress, concludes that somebody has upset the inkstand thereon, differ in any way from that by which Adams and Leverrier discovered a new planet.* The man of science, in fact, simply uses with scrupulous exactness the methods which we all habitually and at every moment use carelessly."

* Lay Sermons, p. 78.

CHAP. II.

Application of his remarks to law of evidence.

These observations are capable of an inverse application. If we wish to apply the methods in question to the investigation of matters of every-day occurrence, with a greater degree of exactness than is commonly needed, it is necessary to know something of the theory on which they rest. This is specially important when, as in judicial proceedings, it is necessary to impose conditions by positive law upon such investigations. On the other hand, when such conditions have been imposed, it is difficult to understand their importance or their true significance, unless the theory on which they are based is understood. It appears necessary for these reasons to enter to a certain extent upon the general subject of the investigation of the truth as to matters of fact, before attempting to explain and discuss that particular branch of it which relates to judicial proceedings.

General object of science.

First, then, what is the general problem of science? It is to discover, collect, and arrange true propositions about facts. Simple as the phrase appears, it is necessary to enter upon some illustration of its terms, namely, (1) facts, (2) propositions, (3) the truth of propositions.

Facts.

First, then, what are facts?

During the whole of our waking life we are in a state of perception. Indeed, consciousness and perception are two names for one thing, according as we regard it from the passive or active point of view, We are conscious of everything that we perceive, and we perceive whatever we are conscious of. Moreover, our perceptions are distinct from each other, some both in space and time, as is the case with all our perceptions of the external world; others, in time only, as is the case with our perceptions of the thoughts and feelings of our own minds.

External facts.

Whatever may be the objects of our perceptions, they make up collectively the whole sum of our thoughts and feelings. They constitute, in short, the world with which we are acquainted, for without entering upon the question of the existence of the external world, it may be asserted with confidence that our knowledge of it is composed, *first*, of our perceptions; and, *secondly*, of the inferences which we draw from them as to what we should perceive if we were favourably situated for that purpose. The human body supplies an illustration of this. No one doubts that his own body is composed not only of the external organs which he perceives by his senses, but of numerous internal organs, most of which it is highly improbable that either he nor any one else will ever see or touch, and some of which he never can, from the nature of things, see or touch as long as he lives. When he affirms the existence of these organs, say the brain or the heart, what he means is that he is led to believe from what he has been told by other persons about human bodies, or observed himself in other human bodies, that if his skull and chest were laid open, those organs would be perceived by the senses of persons who might direct their senses towards them.

Internal facts.

There is another class of perceptions, transient in their duration, and not perceived by the five best marked senses, which are, nevertheless, distinctly perceptible and of the utmost importance. These are thoughts and feelings. Love, hatred, anger, intention, will, wish, knowledge, opinion, are all perceived by the person who feels them. When it is affirmed that a man *is angry*, that he *intends* to sell an estate, that he *knows* the meaning of a word, that he struck a blow *voluntarily* and not by accident, each proposition relates to a matter capable of being as directly perceived as a noise or a flash of light. The only difference between the two classes of propositions is this. When it is affirmed that a man has a given intention, the matter affirmed is one which he and he only can perceive; when it is affirmed that a man is sitting or standing, the matter affirmed is one which may be perceived not only by the man himself, but by any other person able to see, and favourably situated for the purpose. But the circumstance that either event is regarded as being, or as having been, capable of being perceived by some one or other, is what we mean, and all that we mean, when we say that it

CHAP. II. exists or existed, or when we denote the same thing by calling it a fact. The word 'fact' is sometimes opposed to theory sometimes to opinion, sometimes to feeling, but all these modes of using it are more or less rhetorical. When it is used with any degree of accuracy it implies something which exists, and it is as difficult to attach any meaning to the assertion that a thing exists which neither is, nor under any conceivable circumstances could be perceived by any sentient being, as to attach any meaning to the assertion that anything which can be so perceived does not, or at the time of perception did not, exist.

Definition of facts in Evidence Act.

It is with reference to this that the word 'fact' is defined in the Evidence Act (§ 3) as meaning and including—

(1) Any thing, state of things, or relation of things capable of being perceived by the senses, and

(2) Any mental condition of which any person is conscious.

It is important to remember, with respect to facts, that as all thought and language contains a certain element of generality, it is always possible to describe the same facts with greater or less minuteness, and to decompose every fact with which we are concerned into a number of subordinate facts. Thus we might speak of the presence of several persons in a room at one time as a fact, but if the fact were doubted, or if other circumstances rendered it desirable, their respective positions, their occupations, the position of the furniture, and many other particulars might have to be specified.

Propositions.

Such being the nature of facts, what is the meaning of a proposition? A proposition is a collection of words so related as to raise in the minds of those who understand them a corresponding group of images or thoughts.

The characteristic by which words are distinguished from other sounds is their power of producing corresponding thoughts or images. I say thoughts *or* images, because though most words raise what may be intelligibly called images in the mind, this is true principally of those which relate to visible objects. Such words as 'hard,' 'soft,' 'taste,' 'smell,' call up sufficiently definite thoughts, but they can hardly be described as images, and the same is still more true of words which qualify others, like 'although,' 'whereas,' and other adverbs, prepositions and conjunctions.

Illustrations.

The statement that a proposition, in order to be entitled to the name, must raise in the mind a distinct group of thoughts or images, may be explained by two illustrations. The words 'that horse is *niger*' form a proposition to every one who knows that *niger* means black, but to no one else. The words 'I see a sound' form a proposition to no one, unless some signification is attached to the word 'sound' (for instance, an arm of the sea) which would make the words intelligible.

True propositions.

Such being a proposition, what is a true proposition? A true proposition is one which excites in the mind thoughts or images corresponding to those which would be excited in the mind of a person so situated as to be able to perceive the facts to which the proposition relates. The words 'a man is riding down the road on a white horse' form a proposition, because they raise in the mind a distinct group of images. The proposition is true if all persons favourably situated for purposes of observation did actually perceive a corresponding group of facts.

How true propositions are to be framed.

The next question is, How are we to proceed in order to ascertain whether any given proposition about facts is true, and in order to frame true propositions about facts? This, as already observed, is the general problem of science, which is only another name for knowledge so arranged as to be easily understood and remembered.

Facts must be correctly observed and properly recorded.

The facts, in the first place, must be correctly observed. The observations made must, in the next place, be recorded in apt language, and each of these operations is one of far greater delicacy and difficulty than is usually supposed; for it is almost impossible to discriminate between observation and inference, or to make language a bare record of our perceptions, instead of being a running commentary upon them. To

CHAP. II. go into these and some kindred points would extend this inquiry beyond all reasonable bounds, and I accordingly pass them over with this slight reference to their existence. Assuming, then, the existence of observation and language sufficiently correct for common purposes, how are they to be applied to inquiries into matters of fact?

Mr. Mill's theory of logic;—a fixed order prevails in the world.

An answer to these questions sufficient for the present purpose will be supplied by giving a short account of what is said on the subject by Mr. Mill in his treatise on logic. The substance of that part of it which bears upon the present subject is as follows: The first great lesson learnt from the observation of the world in which we live, is that a fixed order prevails amongst the various facts of which it is composed. Under given conditions, fire always burns wood, lead always sinks in water, day always follows night, and night day, and so on. By degrees we are able to learn what the conditions are under which these and other such events happen. We learn, for instance, that the presence of a certain quantity of air is a condition of combustion; that the presence of the force of gravitation, the absence of any equal or greater force acting in an opposite direction, and the maintenance by the water of its properties as a fluid, are conditions necessary to the sinking of lead in water; that the maintenance by the heavenly bodies of their respective positions, and the persistency of the various forces by which their paths are determined, are the conditions under which day and night succeed each other.

Induction and deduction.

The great problem is to find out what particular antecedents and consequents are thus connected together, and what are the conditions of their connection. For this purpose two processes are employed, namely, induction and deduction. Deduction assumes and rests upon previous inductions, and derives a great part at least of its value from the means which it affords of carrying on the process of thought from the point at which induction stops. The questions, What is the ultimate foundation of induction? Why are we justified in believing that all men will die because we have reason to believe that all men hitherto have died? Or that every particle of matter whatever will continue to attract every other particle of matter with a force bearing a certain fixed proportion to its mass and its distance, because other particles of matter have hitherto been observed to do so? are questions which lie beyond the limits of the present inquiry. For practical purposes it is enough to assume that such inferences are valid, and will be found by experience to yield true results in the shape of general propositions, from which we can argue downwards to particular cases according to the rules of verbal logic.

Mere observation of facts insufficient.

True general propositions, however, cannot be extracted directly from the observation of nature or of human conduct, as every fact which we can observe, however apparently simple, is in reality so intricate that it would give us little or no information unless it were connected with and checked by other facts. What, for instance, can appear more natural and simple than the following facts? A tree is cut down. It falls to the ground. Several birds which were perched upon it fly away. Its fall raises a cloud of dust which is dispersed by the wind, and splashes up some of the water in a pond. Natural and simple as this seems, it raises the following questions at least. Why did the tree fall at all? The tree falling, why did not the birds fall too, and how came they to fly away? What became of the dust, and why did it disappear in the air, whereas the water fell back into the pond from which it was splashed? To see in all these facts so many illustrations of the rules by which we can calculate the force of gravity, and the action of fluids on bodies immersed in them is the problem of science in general, and of induction and deduction in particular.

Proceeding of induction.

Generally speaking, this problem is solved by comparing together different groups of facts resembling each other in some particulars, and differing in others, and the different inductive methods described by Mr. Mill are in reality no

CHAP. II. more than rules for arranging these comparisons. The methods which he enumerates are five,* but the three last are little more than special applications of the other two, the method of agreement and the method of difference. Indeed the method of agreement is inconclusive, unless it is applied upon such a scale as to make it equivalent to the method of difference..

Methods of agreement and difference.

The nature of these methods is as follows:—

All events may be regarded as effects of antecedent causes.

Every effect is preceded by a group of events, one or more of which are its true cause or causes, and all of which are possible causes.

The problem is to discriminate between the possible and the true causes.

If whenever the effect occurs one possible cause occurs, the other possible causes varying, the possible cause which is constant is probably the true cause, and the strength of this probability is measured by the persistency with which the one possible cause recurs, and the extent to which the other possible causes vary. Arguments founded on such a state of things are arguments on the method of agreement.

If the effect occurs when a particular set of possible causes precedes its occurrence, and does not occur when the same set of possible causes co-exist, one only being absent, the possible cause which was present when the effect was produced, and was absent when it was not produced, is the true cause of the effect. Arguments founded on such a state of things are arguments on the method of difference.

Illustrations.

The following illustration makes the matter plain. Various materials are mixed together on several occasions. In each case soap is produced, and in each case oil and alkali are two of the materials so mixed. It is probable from this

* 1. The method of agreement. 2. The method of difference. 3. The joint method of agreement and difference. 4. The method of residues. 5. The method of concomitant variations.

that oil and alkali are the causes of the soap, and the degree, of the probability is measured by the number of the experiments and the variety of the ingredients other than oil and alkali. This is the method of agreement.

Various materials, of which oil and alkali are two, are mixed, and soap is produced. The same materials, with the exception of the oil and alkali, are mixed, and soap is not produced. The mixture of the oil and alkali is the cause of the soap. This is the method of difference. The case would obviously be the same if oil and alkali only were mixed. Soap was unknown, and upon the mixture being made, other things being unchanged, soap came into existence.

Difficulties—Several causes producing the same effect—result as to method of agreement.

These are the most important of the rules of induction; but induction is only one step towards the solution of the problems which nature presents. In the statement of the rules of induction it is assumed for the sake of simplicity that all the causes and all the effects under examination are separate and independent facts, and that each cause is connected with some one single effect. This, however, is not the case. A given effect may be produced by any one of several causes. Various causes may contribute to the production of a single effect. This is peculiarly important in reference to the method of agreement. If that method is applied to a small number of instances, its value is small. For instance, other substances might produce soap by their combination besides oil and alkali, say, for instance, that the combination of A and B, and that of C and D would do so. Then, if there were two experiments as follows:

(1) oil and alkali, A and B, produce soap.
(2) oil and alkali, C and D, produce soap.

soap would be produced in each case, but whether by the combination of oil and alkali, or by the combination of A and B, or by that of C and D, or by the combination of oil, or of alkali, with A, B, C or D, would be altogether uncertain.

A watch is stolen, from a place to which A, B, and C only

CHAP. II. had access. Another watch is stolen from another place to which A, D, and E only had access.

In each instance, A is one of three persons one of whom must have stolen the watch, but this is consistent with it having been stolen by any of the other persons mentioned.

Weakness of the method of agreement how cured.

This weakness of the method of agreement can be cured only by so great a multiplication of instances as to make it highly improbable that any other antecedent than the one present in every instance could have caused the effect present in every instance.

For the statement of the theory of chances and its bearing on the probability of events, I must refer those who wish to pursue the subject to the many works which have been written upon it; but its general validity will be inferred by every one from the common observation of life. If it was certain that either A or B, A or C, A or D, and so forth, up to A and Z, had committed one of a large number of successive thefts, of the same kind, no one could doubt that A was the thief.

It is extremely difficult, in practice, to apply such a test as this, and the test when applied is peculiarly liable to error, as each separate alternative requires distinct proof. In the case supposed, for instance, it would be necessary to ascertain separately in each of the cases relied upon, first, that a theft had been committed; then, that one of two persons must have committed it; and lastly, that in each case the evidence bore with equal weight upon each of them.

Intermixture of effects and interference of causes with each other.

The intermixture of effects and the interference of causes with each other is a matter of much greater intricacy and difficulty.

It may take place in one of two ways, *viz.*:

(1.) "In the one, which is exemplified by the joint operation of different forces in mechanics, the separate effects of all the causes continue to be produced, but are compounded together, and disappear in one total."

(2.) "In the other, illustrated by the case of chemical action, the separate effects cease entirely, and are succeeded by phenomena altogether different, and governed by different laws."

In the second case the inductive methods already stated may be applied, though it has difficulties of its own to which I need not now refer.

In the first case, *i. e.*, where an effect is not the result of any one cause, but the result of several causes modifying each other's operation, the results cease to be separately discernible. Some cancel each other. Others merge in one sum, and in this case there is often an insurmountable difficulty in tracing by observation any fixed relation whatever between the causes and the effects. A body, for instance, is at rest This may be the effect of the action of two opposite forces exactly counteracting each other, but how are such causes to be inferred from such an effect ?

A balloon ascends into the air. This appears, if it is treated as an isolated phenomenon, to form an exception to the theory of gravitation. It is in reality an illustration of that theory though several concomitant facts and independent theories must be understood and combined together before this can be ascertained.

The difficulty of applying the inductive methods to such cases arises from the fact that they assume the absence of the state of things supposed. The subsequent and antecedent phenomena must be assumed to be capable of specific and separate observation before it can be asserted that a given fact invariably follows another given fact, or that two sets of possible causes resemble each other in every particular with a single exception.

Deductive method.

It is necessary for this reason to resort to the deductive method, the nature of which is as follows : A general proposition established by induction is used as a premiss from which consequences are drawn according to the rules of logic, as to what must follow under particular circumstances. The inference so drawn is compared with the facts observed, and if the result observed agrees with the deduction from the in-

CHAP. II. ductive premiss, the inference is that the phenomenon is explained. The complete method, inductive and deductive, thus involves three steps,—

(1) Establishing the premiss by induction, or what, in practice, comes to the same thing, by a previous deduction resting ultimately upon induction ;

(2) Reasoning according to the rules of logic to a conclusion ;

(3) Verification of the conclusion by observation.

Illustration. The whole process is illustrated by the discovery and proof of the identity of the central force of the solar system with the force of gravity as known on the earth's surface. The steps in it were as follows :—

(1) It was proved by deductions resting ultimately upon inductions that the earth attracts the moon with a force varying inversely as the square of the distance.

This is the first step, the establishment of the premiss by a process resting ultimately upon induction.

(2) The moon's distance from the earth, and the actual amount of her deflexion from the tangent being known, it was ascertained with what rapidity the earth's attraction would cause the moon to fall if she were no further off and no more acted upon by extraneous forces than terrestrial bodies are.

This is the second step, the reasoning, regulated by the rules of logic.

(3) Finally, this calculated velocity being compared with the observed velocity with which all heavy bodies fall by mere gravity towards the surface of the earth (sixteen feet in the first second, forty-eight in the second, and so forth in the ratio of the odd numbers), the two quantities are found to agree.

This is the verification. The facts observed agree with the facts calculated, therefore the true principle of calculation has been taken.

This paraphrase, for it is no more, of Mr. Mill—is I hope,

sufficient to show, in general, the nature of scientific investigation, and the manner in which it aims at framing true propositions about matters of fact. It would be foreign to the present purpose to follow the subject further. Enough has been said to illustrate the general meaning of such words as "proof" and "evidence" in their application to scientific inquiry. Before inquiring into the application of these principles to judicial investigations, it will be convenient to compare the conditions under which judicial and scientific investigations are carried on.

Judicial and scientific inquiries compared—resemblances.

In some essential points they resemble each other. Inquiries into matters of fact, of whatever kind and with whatever object, are, in all cases whatever, inquiries from the known to the unknown, from our present perceptions or our present recollection (which is in itself a present perception) of past perceptions, to what we might perceive, or might have perceived, if we now were, or formerly had been, or hereafter should be, favourably situated for that purpose. They proceed upon the supposition that there is a general uniformity both in natural events and in human conduct; that all events are connected together as cause and effect; and that the process of applying this principle to particular cases, and of specifying the manner in which it works, though a difficult and delicate operation, can be performed.

Differences.

There are, however, several great differences between inquiries which are commonly called scientific, inquiries that is, into the order and course of nature, and inquiries into isolated matters of fact, whether for judicial or historical purposes, or for the purposes of everyday life. These differences must be carefully observed before we can undertake with much advantage the task of applying to the one subject the principles which appear to be true in reference to the other.

First difference as to amount of evidence.

The first difference is, that in reference to isolated events, we can never, or very seldom, perform experiments, but are tied down to a fixed number of relevant facts which can never be increased.

CHAP. II.

In scientific inquiries unlimited.

The great object of physical science is to invent general formulas (perhaps unfortunately called laws) which when ascertained, sum up and enable us to understand the present, and predict the future course of nature. These laws are ultimately deduced by the method already described from individual facts; but any one fact of an infinite number will serve the purpose of a scientific inquirer as well as any other, and in many, perhaps in most, cases, it is possible to arrange facts for the purpose. In order, for instance, to ascertain the force of terrestrial gravity, it was necessary to measure the time occupied by different bodies in falling through given spaces, and every such observation was an isolated fact. If, however, one experiment failed, or was interfered with, if an observation was inaccurate, or if a disturbing cause, as, for instance, the resistance of the atmosphere had not been allowed for, nothing could be easier than to repeat the process; and inferences drawn from any one set of experiments were obviously as much to be trusted as inferences drawn from any other set. Thus, with regard to inquiries into physical nature, relevant facts can be multiplied to a practically unlimited extent, and it may, by the way, be observed that the ease with which this has been assumed in all ages, is a strong argument that the course of nature does impress mankind as being uniform under superficial variations. For many centuries before the modern discoveries in astronomy were made, the motions of the heavenly bodies were carefully observed, and inferences as to their future course were founded upon those observations. Such observations would have been useless and unmeaning, but for the tacit assumption that what they had done in times past, they would continue to do for the future.

In judicial inquiries limited.

In inquiries into isolated events this great resource is not available. Where the object is to decide what happened on a particular occasion, we can hardly ever draw inferences of any value from what happened on similar occasions, because the groups of events which form the subject of historical or judicial inquiry are so intricate that it can scarcely ever be assumed that they will repeat, or that they have repeated themselves. If we wish to know what happened two thousand years ago, when specific quantities of oxygen and hydrogen were combined, under given circumstances, we can obtain complete certainty by repeating the experiment; but the whole course of human history must recur before we could witness a second assassination of Julius Cæsar.

It cannot be increased.

With reference to such events we are tied down inexorably to a certain limited amount of evidence. We know so much of the assassination of Cæsar as has been told us by the historians, who are to us ultimate authorities, and we know no more. Their testimony must be taken subject to all the deductions which experience shows to be necessary in receiving as true, statements made by historical writers on subjects which interest their feelings, and upon the authority of materials which are no longer extant and therefore cannot be weighed or criticized. Unless by some unforeseen accident, new materials on the subject should come to light, a few pages of general history will for ever comprise the whole amount of human knowledge upon this subject, and any doubts about it, whether they arise from inherent improbabilities in the story itself, from differences of detail in the different narratives, or from general considerations as to the untrustworthy character of historians writing on hearsay, and at a considerable distance of time from the events which they relate, are, and must remain for ever, unsolved and insoluble.

Object of scientific inquiries.

Besides this difference as to the quantity of evidence accessible in scientific and historical inquiries, there is a great difference as to the objects to which the inquiries are directed. The object of inquiries into the course of nature is two fold,—the satisfaction of a form of curiosity, which, to those who feel it at all, is one of the most powerful, and which happens also to be one of the most generally useful elements of human nature; and the attainment of practical

CHAP. II. results of very various kinds. Neither of these ends can be attained unless and until the problems stated by nature have been solved: partially it may be, but at all events truly, as far as the solution goes. On the other hand, there is no pressing or immediate necessity for their solution. Every scientific question is always open, and the answer to it may be discovered after vain attempts to discover it have been made for thousands of years, or an answer long accepted may be rejected and replaced by a better answer after an equally long period. In short, in scientific inquiries, absolute truth, or as near an approach to it as can be made, is the one thing needful, and is the constant object of pursuit. So long as any part of his proof remains incomplete, so long as any one ascertained fact does not fit into and exemplify his theory, the scientific inquirer neither is, nor ought to be, satisfied. Until he has succeeded in excluding the possibility of error, he is bound to the extent, at least, of that possibility, to suspend his judgment.

Object of judicial inquiries.

In judicial inquiries (I need not here notice historical inquiries) the case is different. It is necessary for urgent practical purposes to arrive at a decision which, after a definite process has been gone through, becomes final and irreversible. It is obvious that, under these circumstances, the patient suspension of judgment, and the high standard of certainty required by scientific inquirers, cannot be expected. Judicial decisions must proceed upon imperfect materials, and must be made at the risk of error.

Evidence in scientific inquiries trustworthy.

Finally, inquirers into physical science have an additional advantage over those who conduct judicial inquiries, in the fact that the evidence before them, in so far as they have to depend upon oral evidence, is infinitely more trustworthy than that which is brought forward in courts of justice. The reasons of this are manifold. In the first place, the facts which a scientific observer has to report do not affect his passions. In the second place, his evidence about them is not taken at all unless his powers of observation have been more or less trained and can be depended upon. In the third place, he can hardly know what will be the inference from the facts which he observes until his observations have been combined with those of other persons, so that if he were otherwise disposed to misstate them, he would not know what misstatement would serve his purpose. In the fourth place, he knows that his observations will be confronted with others, so that if he is careless or inaccurate, and, *à fortiori,* if he should be dishonest, he would be found out. In the fifth place, the class of facts which he observes are, generally speaking, simple, and he is usually provided with means specially arranged for the purpose of securing accurate observation, and a careful record of its results.

Evidence in judicial inquiries less trustworthy.

The very opposite of all this is true as regards witnesses in a court of justice. The facts to which they testify are, as a rule, facts in which they are more or less interested, and which in many cases excite their strongest passions to the highest degree. The witnesses are very seldom trained to observe any facts or to express themselves with accuracy upon any subject. They know what the point at issue is, and how their evidence bears upon it, so that they can shape it according to the effect which they wish to produce. They are generally so situated that a large part at least of what they say is secure from contradiction, and the facts which they have to observe being in most instances portions of human conduct, are so intricate that even with the best intention on the part of the witness to speak the truth, he will generally be inaccurate, and almost always incomplete, in his account of what occurred.

Advantages of judicial over scientific inquiries.

So far it appears that our opportunities for investigating and proving the existence of isolated facts are much inferior to our opportunities for investigating and proving the formulas which are commonly called the laws of nature. There is, however, something to be said on the other side. Though the evidence available in judicial and historical inquiries is often scanty, and is always fixed in amount, and though the

CHAP. II. facts which form the subject of such inquiries are far more intricate than those which attract the inquirer into physical nature; though the judge and the historian can derive no light from experiments; though, in a word, their apparatus for ascertaining the truth is far inferior to that of which physical inquirers dispose, the task which they have to perform is proportionally easier and less ambitious. It is attended, moreover, by some special facilities which are great helps in performing it satisfactorily.

Maxims more easily appreciated.

The question whether it is in the nature of things possible that general formulas should ever be devised by the aid of which human conduct can be explained and predicted in the short specific manner in which physical phenomena are explained and predicted, has been the subject of great discussion, and is not yet decided; but no one doubts that approximate rules have been framed which are sufficiently precise to be of great service in estimating the probability of particular events. Whether or not any proposition as to human conduct can ever be enunciated, approaching in generality and accuracy to the proposition that the force of gravity varies inversely as the square of the distance, no one would feel disposed to deny that a recent possessor of stolen property who does not explain his possession is probably either the thief or a receiver; or that if a man refuses to produce a document in his possession, the contents of the document are probably unfavourable to him. In inquiries into isolated facts for practical purposes, such rules as these are nearly as useful as rules of greater generality and exactness, though they are of little service when the object is to interpret a series of facts either for practical or theoretical purposes. If, for instance, the question is whether a particular person committed a crime in the course of which he made use of water, knowledge of the facts that there was a pump in his garden, and that water can be drawn from a well by working the pump handle, is as useful as the most perfect knowledge of hydrostatics. But if the question were as to the means by which water could be supplied for a house and field during the year, considerable knowledge of the theory and practice of hydrostatics and of various other subjects might be necessary, and the more extensive the undertaking might be, the wider would be the knowledge required.

Their limitations more easily perceived.

To this it must be added that the approximate rules which relate to human conduct are warranted principally by each man's own experience of what passes in his own mind, corroborated by his observation of the conduct of other persons, which every one is obliged to interpret upon the hypothesis that their mental processes are substantially similar to his own. Experience appears to show that the results given by this process are correct within narrower limits of error than might have been supposed, though the limits are wide enough to leave room for the exercise of a great amount of individual skill and judgment.

This circumstance invests the rules relating to human conduct with a very peculiar character. They are usually expressed with little precision, and stand in need of many exceptions and qualifications, but they are of greater practical use than rough generalizations of the same kind about physical nature, because the personal experience of those by whom they are used readily supplies the qualifications and exceptions which they require. Compare two such rules as these: 'heavy bodies fall to the ground,' 'the recent possessor of stolen goods is the thief.' The rise of a balloon into the air would constitute an unexplained exception to the first of these rules, which might throw doubt upon its truth, but no one would be led to doubt the second by the fact that a shopkeeper doing a large trade had in his till stolen coins shortly after they had been stolen without having stolen them. Every one would see at once that such a case formed one of the many unstated exceptions to the rule. The reason is, that we know external nature only by observation of a neutral, unsympathetic kind, whereas every man knows more of human nature than any general rule on the subject can ever tell him.

CHAP. II.

Judicial problems are simpler than scientific problems.

To these considerations it must be added that to inquire whether an isolated fact exists, is a far simpler problem than to ascertain and prove the rule according to which facts of a given class happen. The inquiry falls within a smaller compass. The process is generally deductive. The deductions depend upon previous inductions, of which the truth is generally recognised, and which (at least in judicial inquiries) generally share in the advantage just noticed of appealing directly to the personal experience and sympathy of the judge. The deductions, too, are, as a rule, of various kinds and so cross and check each other, and thus supply each other's deficiencies.

Illustrations.

For instance, from one series of facts it may be inferred that A had a strong motive to commit a crime, say the murder of B. From an independent set of facts it may be inferred that B died of poison, and from another independent set of facts that A administered the poison of which B died. The question is, whether A falls within the small class of murderers by poison. If he does, various propositions about him must be true, no two of which have any necessary connection, except upon the hypothesis that he is a murderer. In this case three such propositions are supposed to be true, viz., (1) the death of B by poison, (2) the administration of it by A, and (3) the motive for its administration. Each separate proposition, as it is established, narrows the number of possible hypotheses upon the subject. When it is established that B died of poison, innumerable hypotheses which would explain the fact of his death consistently with A's innocence are excluded; when it is proved that A administered the poison of which B died, every supposition, consistent with A's innocence, except those of accident, justification, and the like, are excluded; when it is shown that A had a motive for administering the poison, the difficulty of establishing any one of these hypotheses, *e. g.*, accident, is largely increased, and the number of suppositions consistent with innocence is narrowed in a corresponding degree.

In judicial inquiries parties interested have opportunities to be heard.

This suggests another remark of the highest importance in estimating the real weight of judicial inquiries. It is that such inquiries in all civilized countries are, or at least ought to be, conducted in such a manner as to give every person interested in the result the fullest possible opportunity of establishing the conclusion which he wishes to establish. In the illustration just given A would have at once the strongest motive to explain the fact that he had administered the poison to B and every opportunity to do so. Hence if he failed to do it, he would either be a murderer or else a member of that infinitesimally small class of persons who, having a motive to commit murder, and having administered poison to the person whom they have a motive to murder, are unable to suggest any probable reason for supposing that they did administer it innocently.

Summary of results.

The results of the foregoing inquiry may be shortly summed up as follows:—

I. The problem of discovering the truth in relation to matters which are judicially investigated is a part of the general problem of science,—the discovery of true propositions as to matters of fact.

II. The general solution of this problem is contained in the rules of induction and deduction stated by Mr. Mill, and generally employed for the purpose of conducting and testing the results of inquiries into physical nature.

III. By the due application of these rules facts may be exhibited as standing towards each other in the relation of cause and effect, and we are able to argue from the cause to the effect and from the effect to the cause with a degree of certainty and precision proportionate to the completeness with which the relevant facts have been observed or are accessible.

IV. The leading differences between judicial investigations and inquiries into physical nature are as follows:—

1. In physical inquiries the number of relevant facts is

CHAP. II. generally unlimited, and is capable of indefinite increase by experiments.

In judicial investigations the number of relevant facts is limited by circumstances, and is incapable of being increased.

2. Physical inquiries can be prolonged for any time that may be required in order to obtain full proof of the conclusion reached, and when a conclusion has been reached, it is always liable to review if fresh facts are discovered, or if any objection is made to the process by which it was arrived at.

In judicial investigations it is necessary to arrive at a definite result in a limited time; and when that result is arrived at, it is final and irreversible with exceptions too rare to require notice.

3. In physical inquiries the relevant facts are usually established by testimony open to no doubt, because they relate to simple facts which do not affect the passions, which are observed by trained observers who are exposed to detection if they make mistakes, and who could not tell the effect of misrepresentation, if they were disposed to be fraudulent.

In judicial inquiries the relevant facts are generally complex. They affect the passions in the highest degree. They are testified to by untrained observers who are generally not open to contradiction, and are aware of the bearing of the facts which they allege upon the conclusion to be established.

4. On the other hand, approximate generalizations are more useful in judicial than they are in scientific inquiries, because in the case of judicial inquiries every man's individual experience supplies the qualifications and exceptions necessary to adjust general rules to particular facts, which is not the case in regard to scientific inquiries.

5. Judicial inquiries being limited in extent, the process of reaching as good a conclusion as is to be got out of the materials is far easier than the process of establishing a scientific conclusion with complete certainty, though the conclusion arrived at is less satisfactory.

Judicial inquiries usually produce only a very high degree of probability.

It follows from what precedes that the utmost result that can in any case be produced by judicial evidence is a very high degree of probability. Whether upon any subject whatever more than this is possible—whether the highest form of scientific proof amounts to more than an assertion that a certain order in nature has hitherto been observed to take place, and that if that order continues to take place such and such events will happen, are questions which have been much discussed, but which lie beyond the sphere of the present inquiry. However this may be, the reasons given above show why courts of justice have to be contented with a lower degree of probability than is rightly demanded in scientific investigation. The highest probability at which a court of justice can under ordinary circumstances arrive is the probability that a witness or a set of witnesses affirming the existence of a fact which they say they perceived by their own senses, and upon which they could not be mistaken, tell the truth. It is difficult to measure the value of such a probability against those which the theories of physical inquirers produce, nor would it serve any practical purpose to attempt to do so. It is enough to say that the process by which a comparatively low degree of probability is shown to exist in the one case is identical in principle with that by which a much higher degree of probability is shown to exist in the other case.

Degrees of probability—moral certainty.

The degrees of probability attainable in scientific and in judicial inquiries are infinite, and do not admit of exact measurement or description. Cases might easily be mentioned in which the degree of probability obtained in either is so high, that if there is any degree of knowledge higher in kind than the knowledge of probabilities, it is impossible for any practical purpose to distinguish between the two. Whether any higher degree of assurance is conceivable than that which may easily be obtained of the facts that the earth revolves round the sun, and that Delhi was besieged and taken by the English in 1857, is a question which does not

CHAP. II. belong to this inquiry. For all practical purposes such conclusions as these may be described as absolutely certain. From these down to the faintest guess about the inhabitants of the stars, and the faintest suspicion that a particular person has committed a crime, there is a descending scale of probabilities which does not admit of any but a very rough measurement for practical purposes. The only point in it worth noticing is what is commonly called moral certainty, and this means simply such a degree of probability as a prudent man would act upon under the circumstances in which he happens to be placed in reference to the matter of which he is said to be morally certain.

Moral certainty is a question of prudence.

What constitutes moral certainty is thus a question of prudence, and not a question of calculation. It is commonly said in reference to judicial inquiries, that in criminal cases guilt ought to be proved "beyond all reasonable doubt," and that in civil cases the decision ought to be in favour of the side which is most probably right. To the latter part of this rule there is no objection, though it should be added that it cannot be applied absolutely without reserve. For instance, a civil case in which character is at stake partakes more or less of the nature of a criminal proceeding; but the first part of the rule means nothing more than that in most cases the punishment of an innocent man is a great evil, and ought to be carefully avoided; but that, on the other hand, it is often impossible to eliminate an appreciable though undefinable degree of uncertainty from the decision that a man is guilty. The danger of punishing the innocent is marked by the use of the expression "no doubt," the necessity of running some degree of risk of doing so in certain cases is intimated by the word "reasonable." The question, what sort of doubt is "reasonable" in criminal cases is a question of prudence. Hardly any case ever occurs in which it is not possible for an ingenious person to suggest hypotheses consistent with the prisoner's innocence. The hypothesis of falsehood on the part of the witnesses can never be said to be more than highly improbable.

Principle of estimating probabilities is that of Mr. Mill's method of difference.

Though it is impossible to invent any rule by which different probabilities can be precisely valued, it is always possible to say whether or not they fulfil the conditions of what Mr. Mill describes as the Method of Difference; and if not, how nearly they approach to fulfilling it. The principle is precisely the same in all cases, however complicated or however simple, and whether the nature of the inquiry is scientific or judicial. In all cases the known facts must be arranged and classified with reference to the different hypotheses, or unknown or suspected facts, by which the existence of the known facts can be accounted for. If every hypothesis except one is inconsistent with one or more of the known facts, that one hypothesis is proved. If more than one hypothesisis consistent with the known facts, but one only is reasonably probable—that is to say, if one only is in accordance with the common course of events, that one in judicial inquiries may be said to be proved "beyond all reasonable doubt." The word "reasonable" in this sentence denotes a fluctuating and uncertain quantity of probability (if the expression may be allowed), and shows that the ultimate question in judicial proceedings is and must be in most cases a question of prudence.

Illustration.

Let the question be whether A did a certain act; the circumstances are such that the act must have been done by somebody, but it can have been done only by A or by B. If A and B are equally likely to have done the act, the matter cannot be carried further, and the question Who did it? must remain undecided. But if the act must have been done by one person, if it required great physical strength, and if A is an exceedingly powerful man and B a child, it may be said to be proved that B did it. If A is stronger than B, but the disproportion between their strength is less, it is probable that A did it, but not impossible that B may have done it, and so on. In such a case as this a nearer approach than usual to a distinct measurement of the probability is possible, but no complete and definite statement on the subject can be made.

Judicial inquiries involve two classes of inferences.

Such being the general nature of the object towards which judicial inquiries are directed, and the general nature of the process by which they are carried on, it will be well to examine the chief forms of that process somewhat more particularly.

It will be found upon examination that the inferences employed in judicial inquiries fall under two heads:—

(1) Inferences from an assertion, whether oral or documentary, to the truth of the matter asserted.

(2) Inferences from facts which, upon the strength of such assertions, are believed to exist, to facts of which the existence has not been so asserted.

For the sake of simplicity, I do not here distinguish various subordinate classes of inferences, such as inferences from the manner in which assertions are made, from silence, from the absence of assertion, and from the conduct of the parties. They may be regarded as so many forms of assertion, and may therefore be classed under the general head of inferences from an assertion to the truth of the matter asserted.

Direct and circumstantial evidence.

This is the distinction usually expressed by saying that all evidence is either direct or circumstantial. I avoid the use of this expression, partly because, as I have already observed, direct *evidence* means direct assertion, whereas circumstantial *evidence* means a fact on which an inference is to be founded, and partly for the more important reason that the use of the expression favours an unfounded notion that the principles on which the two classes of inferences depend are different, and that they have different degrees of cogency, which admit of comparison. The truth is that each inference depends upon precisely the same general theory, though somewhat different considerations apply to the investigation of cases in which the facts testified to are many, and to cases in which the facts testified to are few.

The general theory has been already stated. In every case the question is, are the known facts inconsistent with any other than the conclusion suggested? The known facts in every case whatever are the evidence in the narrower sense of the word. The judge hears with his own ears the statements of the witnesses and sees with his own eyes the documents produced in court. His task is to infer, from what he thus sees and hears, the existence of facts which he neither sees nor hears.

Illustration.

Let the question be whether a will was executed. Three witnesses, entirely above suspicion, come and testify that they witnessed its execution. These assertions are facts which the judge hears for himself. Now there are three possible suppositions, and no more, which the judge has to consider in proceeding from the known fact, the assertion of the witnesses that they saw the will executed, to the fact to be proved—the actual execution of the will:—

(1) The witnesses may be speaking the truth.

(2) The witnesses may be mistaken.

(3) The witnesses may be telling a falsehood.

The circumstances may be such as to render suppositions (2) and (3) improbable in the highest degree, and generally speaking they would be so. In such a case the first hypothesis, *i.e.*, that the will really was executed as alleged, would be proved. The facts before the judge would be inconsistent with any other reasonable hypothesis except that of the execution of the will. This would be commonly called a case of direct evidence.

Let the question be whether A committed a crime. The facts which the judge actually knows are that certain witnesses made before him a variety of statements which he believes to be true. The result of these statements is to establish certain facts which show that either A or B or C must have committed the crime, and that neither B nor C did commit it. In this case the facts before the judge would be inconsistent with any other reasonable hypothesis except that A committed the crime. This would be commonly called a case of circumstantial evidence; yet it is obvious that the principle on which the investigation proceeds as in the

CHAP. II. last case is identically the same. The only difference is in the number of inferences, but no new principle is introduced.

Identity of this process with Mr. Mill's theory.

It is also clear that each case is identical in principle with the method of difference as explained by Mr. Mill.

Mr. Mill's illustration of the application of that method to the motions of the planets is as follows:—The planets with a central force give areas proportional to the times. The planets without a central force give a different set of motions; but areas proportional to the times are observed. Therefore there is a central force.

Similarly in the cases suggested. The assertions of the witnesses give the execution of a will, *i. e.*, no other cause can account for those assertions having been made. If the will had not been executed those assertions would not have been made. But the assertions were made. Therefore the will was executed.

Though inferences from an assertion to its truth, and inferences from facts taken as true to other facts not asserted to be true, rest upon the same principle, each inference has its peculiarities.

Inference from assertion to matter asserted.

The inference from the assertion to the truth of the matter asserted is usually regarded as an easy matter, calling for little remark.

Though in particular cases it is really easy, and though in a certain sense it is always easy, to deal with, to deal with it rightly, is by far the most difficult task which falls to the lot of a judge and miscarriages of justice are almost invariably caused by dealing with it wrongly. This requires full explanation.

To infer from an assertion the truth of the matter asserted, is in one sense the easiest thing in the world. The intellectual process consists of only one step, and that is a step which gives no trouble, and is taken in most cases unconsciously. But to draw the inference in those cases only in which it is true is a matter of the utmost difficulty. If we were able to affirm the proposition, "All men upon all occasions speak the truth," the remaining propositions,—"This man says so and so," "Therefore it is true," would present no difficulty. The major premiss, however, is subject to wide exceptions, which are not forced upon the judge's attention. Moreover, if they were, the judge has often no means of ascertaining whether or not, and to what extent they apply to any particular case.

Its difficulties.

How is it possible to tell how far the powers of observation and memory of a man seen once for a few minutes enable him, and how far the innumerable motives by any one or more of which he may be actuated dispose him, to tell the truth upon the matter on which he testifies? Cross-examination supplies a test to a certain extent, but those who have seen most of its application will be disposed to trust it least as a proof that a man not shaken by it ought to be believed. A cool, steady liar who happens not to be open to contradiction will baffle the most skilful cross-examiner in the absence of accidents, which are not so common in practice as persons who take their notions on the subject from anecdotes or fiction would suppose.

Cannot be affected by rules of evidence.

No rules of evidence which the legislator can enact can perceptibly affect this difficulty. Judges must deal with it as well as they can by the use of their natural faculties and acquired experience, and the miscarriages of justice in which they will be involved by reason of it must be set down to the imperfection of our means of arriving at truth. The natural and acquired shrewdness and experience by which an observant man forms an opinion as to whether a witness is or is not lying, is by far the most important of all a judge's qualifications, infinitely more important than any acquaintance with law or with rules of evidence. No trial ever occurs in which the exercise of this faculty is not required; but it is only in exceptional cases that questions arise which present any legal difficulty, or in which it is necessary to exercise any particular ingenuity in putting together the different facts which the evidence tends to establish. This pre-eminently important power for a judge is not to be learnt out of books.

CHAP. II. In so far as it can be acquired at all, it is to be acquired only by experience, for the acquisition of which the position of a judge is by no means peculiarly favourable. People come before him with their cases ready prepared, and give the evidence which they have determined to give. Unless he knows them in their unrestrained and familiar moments, he will have great difficulty in finding any good reason for believing one man rather than another. The rules of evidence may provide tests, the value of which has been proved by long experience, by which judges may be satisfied that the quality of the materials upon which their judgments are to proceed is not open to certain obvious objections; but they do not profess to enable the judges to know whether or not a particular witness tells the truth or what inference is to be drawn from a particular fact. The correctness with which this is done must depend upon the natural sagacity, the logical power, and the practical experience of the judge, not upon his acquaintance with the law of evidence.

Grounds for believing and disbelieving a witness.

Power.

The grounds for believing or disbelieving particular statements made by particular people under particular circumstances may be brought under three heads,—those which affect the power of the witness to speak the truth; those which affect his will to do so; and those which arise from the nature of the statement itself and from surrounding circumstances. A man's power to speak the truth depends upon his knowledge and his power of expression. His knowledge depends partly on his accuracy in observation, partly on his memory, partly on his presence of mind; his power of expression depends upon an infinite number of circumstances, and varies in relation to the subject of which he has to speak.

Will.

A man's will to speak the truth depends upon his education, his character, his courage, his sense of duty, his relation to the particular facts as to which he is to testify, his humour for the moment, and a thousand other circumstances, as to the presence or absence of which in any particular case it is often difficult to form a true opinion.

CHAP. II.

The third set of reasons are those which depend upon the probability of the statement.

Proba-bility of statement.

Many discussions have taken place on the effect of the improbability of a statement upon its credibility in cases which can never fall under judicial consideration. It is unnecessary to enter upon that subject here. Looking at the matter merely in relation to judicial inquiries, it is sufficient to observe that whilst the improbability of a statement is always a reason, and may be, in practice, a conclusive reason for disbelieving it, its probability is a poor reason for believing it if it rests upon uncorroborated testimony. Probable falsehoods are those which an artful liar naturally tells; and the fact that a good opportunity for telling such a falsehood occurs is the commonest of all reasons for its being told.

Expe-rience is the only guide on the subject.

Upon the whole, it must be admitted that little that is really serviceable can be said upon the inference from an assertion to the truth of the matter asserted. The observations of which the matter admits are either generalities too vague to be of much practical use, or they are so narrow and special that they can be learnt only by personal observation and practical experience. Such observations are seldom, if ever thrown by those who make them into the form of express propositions. Indeed, for obvious reasons, it would be impossible to do so. The most acute observer would never be able to catalogue the tones of voice, the passing shades of expression or the unconscious gestures which he had learnt to associate with falsehood; and if he did, his observations would probably be of little use to others. Every one must learn matters of this sort for himself, and though no sort of knowledge is so important to a judge, no rules can be laid down for its acquisition.*

* I may give a few anecdotes which have no particular value in themselves, but which show what I mean. "I always used to look at the witnesses' toes when I was cross-examining them," said a friend of mine who had practised at the bar in Ceylon. "As soon as they began to lie they always fidgeted about with them." I knew a

CHAP. II.

Illustration.

If the opinion here advanced appears strange, I would invite attention to the following illustration:—Is there any class of cases in which it is, in practice, so difficult to come to a satisfactory decision as those which depend upon the explicit, direct testimony of a single witness uncorroborated, and, by the nature of the case, incapable of corroboration? For instance, a man and a woman are travelling alone in a railway carriage. The train stops at a station, and the woman charges the man with indecent conduct, which he denies. Nothing particular is known about the character or previous history of either. The woman is not betrayed on cross-examination into any inconsistency. There are no cases in which the difficulty of arriving at a satisfactory decision is anything like so great. It is easy to decide them as it is easy to make a bet, but it is easier to deal satisfactorily with the most complicated and lengthy chain of inference.

The uncertainty of inferences from an assertion to the truth of the matter asserted may be shown by stating them logically. They may be considered as being the conclusions of syllogisms in this form:—

Judge who formed the opinion that a letter had been forged because the expression "that woman" which it contained appeared to him to be one which a woman and not a man would use, and the question was whether the letter in question had been forged by a woman. In the Life of Lord Keeper Guildford it is said that he always acted on the principle that a man was to be believed in what he said when he was in a passion. The commonplaces about the evidence of policemen, children, women, and the natives of particular countries belong to this subject. The only remark I feel inclined to add to what is commonly said on it is that, according to my observation, the power to tell the truth, which implies accurate observation, knowledge of the relative importance of facts, and power of description, properly proportioned to each other, is much less common than people usually suppose it to be. It is extremely difficult for an untrained person not to mix up inference and assertion. It is also difficult for such a person to distinguish between what they themselves saw and heard and what they were told by others, unless their attention is specially directed to the distinction.

All men situated in such and such a manner speak the truth or speak falsely (as the case may be).

A B, situated in such and such a manner, says so and so.

Therefore, in saying so and so, he speaks truly or falsely (as the case may be).

This is a deduction resting on a previous induction, and it is obvious that the induction which furnishes the major premiss must always be exceedingly imperfect, and that the truth of the minor premiss which is essential to the deduction is always more or less conjectural.

Inference from facts proved to facts not otherwise proved.

In many cases the defects of inferences of the first kind may be incidentally remedied by inferences of the second kind, namely, inferences from facts which are asserted, and, on the ground of such assertion, believed by the court to exist, to facts not asserted to exist; and these I now proceed to examine.

Inference from assertion to truth sometimes really easy.

I have observed that the inference from an assertion to the truth of the matter asserted often is as easy as it always appears to be. In very many instances, which it is much easier to recognise when they occur than to reduce to rule, a direct assertion, even by a single witness of whom little is known, is entitled to great weight. Suppose, for instance, that the matter asserted is of a character indifferent in itself, and upon which the witness is, or for aught he can tell may be, open to contradiction. A single assertion of this sort may outweigh a mass of artfully combined falsehood. Suppose, for instance, that a number of witnesses have been called to prove an *alibi*, and that they allege that on a given day they were all present together with the person on behalf of whom the *alibi* is to be proved at a fair held at a certain place. If the magistrate of the district, whose duty it was to superintend the fair, were to depose that the fair did not begin to be held till a day subsequent to the one in question, no one would doubt that the witnesses had conspired together to give false evidence by the familiar trick of changing the day. In this case one direct assertion would outweigh many direct asser-

CHAP. II. tions. Why? Because the magistrate of the district would be a man of character and position; because he would (we must assume) be quite indifferent to the particular case in issue; because he would be deposing to a fact of which it would be his official duty to be cognizant, and on which he could hardly be mistaken; and lastly, because the fact would be known to a vast number of people, and he would be open to contradiction, detection, and ruin if he spoke falsely. Change these circumstances, and the equally explicit testimony of the very same man might be worthless. Suppose, for instance, that he was asked whether he had committed adultery? His denial would carry hardly any weight in any conceivable case, inasmuch as the charge is one which a guilty man would always deny, and an innocent man could do no more. In other words, since the course of conduct supposed is one which a man would certainly take whether he were innocent or not, the fact of his taking it would afford no criterion as to his guilt or innocence.

Now in almost all judicial proceedings a certain number of facts are established by direct assertions made under such circumstances that no one would seriously doubt their truth. Others are rendered probable in various degrees, and thus the judge is furnished with facts which he may use as a basis for his inferences as to the existence of other facts which are either not asserted to exist or are asserted to exist, by unsatisfactory witnesses.

Such inferences comparatively easy.

These inferences are generally considered to be more difficult to draw than the inference from an assertion to the matter asserted. In fact, it is far easier to combine materials supposed to be sound, than to ascertain that they are sound. In the one case no rules for the judge's guidance can be laid down. No process is gone through, the correctness of which can afterwards be independently tested. The judge has nothing to trust to but his own natural and acquired sagacity. In the other case all that is required is to go through a process with which, as Mr. Huxley remarks, every one has a general superficial acquaintance tested by every-day practice, and the theory of which it is easy to understand and interesting to follow out and apply.

Facts must fulfil test of method of difference.

The facts supposed to be proved must ultimately fulfil the conditions of the method of difference, but they may be combined by any of the recognised logical methods, or by a combination of them all. The object, indeed, at which they are all directed is the same, though they reach it by different roads. A few illustrations will make this plain. The question is, whether A has embezzled a small sum of money, say a particular rupee which he received on account of his employer, and did not enter in a book in which he ought to have entered it. His defence is that the omission to make the entry was accidental. The account-book is examined, and it is found that in a long series of instances omissions of small sums have been made, each of which omissions is in A's favour. This, in the absence of explanation, would leave no reasonable doubt of A's guilt in each and every case. It would be practically impossible to account for such facts except upon the assumption of systematic fraud. Logically, this is an instance of the Method of Agreement applied to so great a number of instances as to exclude the operation of chance. When, however, this is done, the Method of Agreement becomes a case of the Method of Difference.

Converging probabilities.

The well-known cases in which guilt is inferred from a number of separate, independent, and, so to speak, converging probabilities, may be regarded as an illustration of the same principle. Their general type is as follows :—

B was murdered by some one.

Whoever murdered B had a motive for his murder.

A had a motive for murdering B.

Whoever murdered B had an opportunity for murdering B.

A had an opportunity for murdering B.

Whoever murdered B made preparations for the murder of B.

CHAP. II.

A acted in a manner which might amount to a preparation for murdering B.

In each of these instances, which might of course be indefinitely multiplied, one item of agreement is established between the ascertained fact that B was murdered and the hypothesis that A murdered him; and it does sometimes happen that these coincidences may be multiplied to such an extent and may be of such a character as to exclude the supposition of chance, and justify the inference that A was guilty.* The case, however, is a rare one, and there is always a great risk of injustice unless the facts proved go beyond the mere multiplication of circumstances separately indicating guilt, and amount to a substantial exclusion of every reasonable possibility of innocence.

Illustration.

The celebrated passage in Lord Macaulay's Essays in which he seeks to prove that Sir Philip Francis was the author of Junius's letters, is an instance of an argument of this kind. The letters, he says, show that five facts can be predicated of Junius, whoever he may have been. But these five facts may also be predicated of Sir Philip Francis and of no one else. Whether any part of this argument can in fact be sustained, is a question to which it would be impertinent to refer here, but that the method on which it proceeds is legitimate there can be no doubt.

Rule as to corpus delicti.

The cases in which it is most probable that injustice will be done by the application of the method of agreement to judicial inquiries are those in which the existence of the principal fact has to be inferred from circumstances pointing to it. This is the foundation of the well-known rule that the *corpus delicti* should not in general in criminal cases be inferred from other facts, but should be proved independently. It has been sometimes narrowed to the proposition that no one should be convicted of murder unless the body of the murdered person has been discovered.

* See Richardson's Case, p. 68.

CHAP. II.

Neither of these rules is more than a rough and partial application of the general principle stated above. If the circumstances are such as to make it morally certain (within the definition given above) that a crime has been committed, the inference that it was so committed is as safe as any other such inference.

Illustrations.

The captain of a ship, a thousand miles from any land, and with no other vessel in sight, is seen to run into his cabin, pursued by several mutinous sailors. The noise of a struggle and a splash are heard. The sailors soon afterwards come out of the cabin and take the command of the vessel. The cabin windows are open. The cabin is in confusion, and the captain is never seen or heard of again.

A person looks at his watch and returns it to his pocket. Immediately afterwards a man comes past, and makes a snatch at the watch, which disappears. The man being pursued, runs away and swims across a river; he is arrested on the other side. He has no watch in his possession, and the watch is never found.

In these cases it is morally certain that murder and theft respectively were committed, though in the first case the body, and in the second the watch is not producible.

Existency of corpus delicti sometimes wrongly inferred.

Cases, however, do undoubtedly occur in which the inference that a crime has been committed at all is a mistake. They may often be resolved into a case of begging the question. The process is this: suspicion that a crime has been committed is excited, and upon inquiry a number of circumstances are discovered which if it is assumed that a crime has been committed are suspicious, but which are not suspicious unless that assumption is made.

A ship is cast away under such circumstances that her loss may be accounted for either by fraud or by accident. The captain is tried for making away with her. A variety of circumstances exist which would indicate preparation and expectation on his part if the ship really was made away with, but which would justify no suspicion at all if she

CHAP. II. was not. It is manifestly illogical first to regard the antecedent circumstances as suspicious, because the loss of the ship is assumed to be fraudulent, and next to infer that the ship was fraudulently destroyed from the suspicious character of the antecedent circumstances. This, however, is a fallacy of very common occurrence, both in judicial proceedings and in common life.*

The modes in which facts may be so combined as to exclude every hypothesis other than the one which it is intended to establish are very numerous, and are, I think, better learnt from specific illustrations and from actual practice than from abstract theories. One of the objects of the illustrations given in the next chapter is to enable students to understand this matter.

Summary of conclusions.

The result of the foregoing inquiries may be summed up as follows:—

I. In judicial inquiries the facts which form the materials for the decision of the court are the facts that certain persons assert certain things under certain circumstances. These facts the judge hears with his own ears. He also sees with his own eyes documents and other things respecting which he hears certain assertions.

II. His task is to infer—

(1) From what he himself hears and sees the existence of the facts asserted to exist;

(2) From the facts which on the strength of such assertions he believes to exist other facts which are not so asserted to exist.

III. Each of these inferences is an inference from the effect to the cause, and each ought to conform to the Method of Difference; that is to say, the circumstances in each case should be such that the effect is inconsistent

* An illustration of this form of error occurred in the case of R. *vs.* Steward and two others, who were convicted at Singapore in 1867 for casting away the Schooner *Erin*, and subsequently received a free pardon on the ground of their innocence.

(subject to the limitations contained in the following paragraphs) with the existence of any other cause for it than the cause of which the existence is proposed to be proved.

IV. The highest result of judicial investigation must generally be, for the reasons already given, to show that certain conclusions are more or less probable.

V. The question—what degree of probability is it necessary to show, in order to warrant a judicial decision in a given case, is a question not of logic but of prudence and is identical with the question, "What risk of error is it wise to run, regard being had to the consequences of error in either direction?"

VI. This degree of probability varies in different cases to an extent which cannot be strictly defined, but wherever it exists it may be called moral certainty.

CHAPTER III.

THE THEORY OF RELEVANCY, WITH ILLUSTRATIONS.

CHAP. III. Relevancy means connection of events as cause and effect.

AN intelligence of sufficient capacity might perhaps be able to conceive of all events as standing to each other in the relation of cause and effect; and though the most powerful of human minds are unequal to efforts which fall infinitely short of this, it is possible not only to trace the connection between cause and effect, both in regard to human conduct and in regard to inanimate matter, to very considerable lengths, but to see that numerous events are connected together, although the precise nature of the links which connect them may not be open to observation. The connection may be traced in either direction, from effect to cause or from cause to effect; and if these two words were taken in their widest acceptation it would be correct to say that when any theory has been formed which alleges the existence of any fact, all facts are relevant which, if that theory was true, would stand to the fact alleged to exist either in the relation of cause or in the relation of effect.

Objections.

It may be said that this theory would extend the limits of relevancy beyond all reasonable bounds, inasmuch as all events whatever are or may be more or less remotely connected by the universal chain of cause and effect, so that the theory of gravitation would upon this principle be relevant wherever one of the facts in issue involved the falling of an object to the ground.

Answer.

The answer to this objection is, that wide, general causes, which apply to all occurrences, are, in most cases, admitted, and do not require proof; but no doubt if their application to the matter in question were doubtful or were misunderstood, it might be necessary to investigate them. For instance, suppose that, in an action for infringing a patent, the defence set up was that the patent was invalid, because the invention had been anticipated by some one who preceded the patentee. The issue might be whether an earlier machine was substantially the same as the patentee's machine. All the facts, therefore, which went to make up each machine would be facts in issue. But each machine would be constructed with reference to the general formulæ called laws of nature, and thus the existence of an alleged law of nature might well become, not merely relevant, but a fact in issue. If, the first inventor of barometers had taken out a patent, and had had to defend its validity, the variation of atmospheric pressure, according to the height of a column of air, and the fact that air has weight, might have been facts in issue.

Traceable influence of causes on effects narrow.

With regard to the remark that all events are connected together more or less remotely as cause and effect, it is to be observed that though this is or may be true, it is equally true that the limit within which the influence of causes upon effects can be perceived is generally very narrow. A knife is used to commit a murder, and it is notched and stained with blood in the process. The knife is carefully washed, the water is thrown away, and the notch in the blade is ground out. It is obvious that, unless each link in this chain of cause and effect could be separately proved, it would be impossible to trace the connection between the knife cleaned and ground and the purpose for which it had been used. On the other hand, if the first step—the fact that the knife was bloody at a given time and place—was proved, there would be no use in inquiring into the further effects produced by that fact, such as the staining of the water in which it was washed, the infinitesimal effects produced on the river into which the water was thrown, and so forth.

Rule as to cause and effects true

The rule, therefore, that facts may be regarded as relevant which can be shown to stand either in the relation of cause or in the relation of effect to the fact to which they are said to

CHAP. III. subject to caution that every step in the connection must be made out.

be relevant, may be accepted as true, subject to the caution that, when an inference is to be founded upon the existence of such a connection, every step by which the connection is made out must either be proved, or be so probable under the circumstances of the case that it may be presumed without proof.

Illustration.

Footmarks are found near the scene of a crime. The circumstances are such that they may be presumed to be the footmarks made by the criminal. These marks correspond precisely with a pair of shoes found on the feet of the accused. The presumption founded upon common experience, though its force may vary indefinitely, is that no two pairs of shoes would make precisely the same marks. It may further be presumed, though this presumption is by no means conclusive, that shoes were worn by their owner on a given occasion. Here the steps are as follows :—

(1) The person who committed the crime probably made those marks by pressing the shoes which he wore on the ground.

(2) The person who committed the crime probably wore his own shoes.

(3) The shoes so pressed were probably these shoes.

(4) These shoes are A B's shoes.

Therefore A B probably made those marks with those shoes.

Therefore A B probably committed the crime.

These facts may be exhibited in the relation of cause and effect thus :—

(1) A's owning the shoes was the cause of his wearing them.

(2) His wearing them at a given place and time caused the marks.

(3) The marks were caused by the flight of the criminal.

(4) The flight of the criminal was caused by the commission of the crime.

(5) Therefore the marks were caused by the flight of A the criminal, after committing the crime.

Obscurity of this definition.

Though this mode of describing relevancy might be correct, it would not be readily understood. For instance, it might be asked, how is an *alibi* relevant under this definition? The answer is, that a man's absence from a given place at a given time is a cause of his not having done a given act at that place and time. This mode of using language would, however, be obscure, and it was for this reason that relevancy was very fully defined in the Evidence Act (ss. 6—11, both inclusive) These sections enumerate specifically the different instances of the connection between cause and effect which occur most frequently in judicial proceedings. They are designedly worded very widely, and in such a way as to overlap each other. Thus a motive for a fact in issue (s. 8) is part of its cause (s. 7). Subsequent conduct influenced by it (s. 8) is part of its effect (s. 7). Facts relevant under s. 11 would, in most cases, be relevant under other sections. The object of drawing the Act in this manner was that the general ground on which facts are relevant might be stated in as many and as popular forms as possible, so that if a fact is relevant, its relevancy may be easily ascertained.

Importance of their sections.

These sections are by far the most important, as they are the most original part of the Evidence Act, as they affirm positively what facts may be proved, whereas the English law assumes this to be known, and merely declares negatively that certain facts shall not be proved.

Important as these sections are for puposes of study, and in order to make the whole body of law to which they belong easily intelligible to students and practitioners not trained in English courts, they are not likely to give rise to litigation or to nice distinctions. The reason is that s. 167 of the Evidence Act which was formerly s. 57 of II. of 1855, renders it practically a matter of little importance whether evidence of a particular fact is admitted or not. The extreme intricacy and minuteness of the law of England on this subject is principally due to the fact that the improper admission or rejection of a single question and answer would give a right to a new trial in a civil case, and would upon a criminal trial be sufficient ground for the quashing of a conviction before the Court for Crown Cases reserved.

The improper admission or rejection of evidence in India has no effect at all unless the court thinks that the evidence improperly dealt with either turned or ought to have turned the scale. A judge, moreover, if he doubts as to the relevancy of a fact suggested, can, if he thinks it will lead to anything relevant, ask about it himself under s. 165.

Illustrations.

In order to exhibit fully the meaning of these sections, to show how the Act was intended to be worked, and to furnish students with models by which they may be guided in the discharge of the most important of their duties, abstracts are appended of the evidence given at the following remarkable trials:—

1. R. *v.* Donellan.
2. R. *v.* Belany.
3. R. *v.* Richardson.
4. R. *v.* Patch.
5. R. *v.* Palmer.

To every fact proved in each of these cases, the most intricate that I could discover, a note is attached, showing under what section of the Evidence Act it would be relevant.

I may observe upon these cases that the general principles of evidence are, perhaps, more clearly displayed in trials for murder, than in any others. Murders are usually concealed with as much care as possible; and, on the other hand, they must, from the nature of the case, leave traces behind them which render it possible to apply the argument from effects to causes with greater force in these than in most other cases. Moreover, as they involve capital punishment and excite peculiar attention, the evidence is generally investigated with special care. There are accordingly few cases which show so distinctly the sort of connection between fact and fact, which makes the existence of one fact a good ground for inferring the existence of another.

I.

Case of R. *v.* Donellan.*

John Donellan, Esq., was tried at Warwick Spring Assizes, 1781, before Mr. Justice Buller, for the murder of Sir Theodosius Broughton, his brother-in-law, a young man of fortune, twenty years of age,[1] who, up to the moment of his death, had been in good health and spirits, with the exception of a trifling ailment, for which he occasionally took a laxative draught.[2] Mrs. Donellan was the sister of the deceased, and, together with Lady Broughton, his mother, lived with him at Lawford Hall, the family mansion.[2]

In the event of Sir T. Broughton's death, unmarried and without issue, the greater part of his fortune would descend to Mrs. Donellan;[3] but it was stated, though not proved, by the prisoner in his defence that he on his marriage entered into articles for the immediate settling of her whole fortune on herself and children, and deprived himself of the possibility of enjoying even a life estate in case of her death, and that this settlement extended not only to the fortune, but to expectancies.[4]

For some time before the death of Sir Theodosius the prisoner had on several occasions falsely represented his health

* Wills, on "Circumstantial Evidence," pp. 192-6.

[1] Introductory fact (section 9).

[2] State of things under which facts in issue happen (section 7).

[3] Motive (section 8).

[4] Fact rebutting an inference suggested by a relevant fact (section 9). These facts are omitted by Mr. Wills, but are mentioned in my account of the case. Gen. View, Crim. Law., p. 338.

to be very bad, and his life to be precarious.[5] On the 29th of August the apothecary in attendance sent him a mild and harmless draught to be taken the next morning.[6] In the evening the deceased was out fishing,[7] and the prisoner told his mother that he had been out with him, and that he had imprudently got his feet wet, both of which assertions were false.[8] When Sir Theodosius was called on the following morning he was in good health,[9] and about seven o'clock his mother went to his chamber to give him his draught,[10] of which he immediately complained,[11] and she remarked that it smelt like bitter almonds.[12] In about two minutes he struggled very much as if to keep the medicine down, and Lady Broughton observed a gurgling in his stomach;[13] in ten minutes he seemed inclined to doze;[13] but in five minutes afterwards she found him with his eyes fixed, his teeth clenched, and froth running out of his mouth, and within half an hour after taking the dose he died.[13]

Lady Broughton ran down-stairs to give orders to a servant to go for the apothecary, who lived about three miles distant,[14] and in less than five minutes after Sir Theodosius had been taken Donellan asked where the physic bottle was, and Lady

[5] Facts showing preparation for facts in issue (section 8). The statements are also admissions as against the prisoner (section 17).

[6] A fact affording an opportunity for facts in issue (section 7).

[7] Introductory to what follows (section 9).

[8] Preparation (section 8). Admission (section 17).

[9] State of things under which fact in issue happened (section 7).

[10] It was suggested that Donellan changed the apothecary's draught for a poisoned one administered by Lady Broughton, an innocent agent. Therefore the administration of the draught suggested to be poisoned was a fact in issue (section 5).

[11] As to this, see section 14.

[12] *I. e.*, of prussic acid. Lady Broughton perceived by smell the presence of the poison. Therefore she smelt a fact in issue (section 5).

[13] Effects of facts in issue (section 7). All these facts go to make up the fact of his death, which was a fact in issue.

[14] Introductory to next fact as fixing the time (section 9).

Broughton showed him the two bottles. The prisoner then took up one of them and said, "Is this it?" and being answered "Yes," he poured some water out of the water bottle which was near into the phial, shook it, and then emptied it into some dirty water which was in a wash-hand basin. Lady Broughton said, "You should not meddle with the bottle," upon which the prisoner snatched up the other bottle and poured water into that also, and shook it, and then put his finger into it and tasted it. Lady Broughton again asked what he was about, and said he ought not to meddle with the bottles; on which he replied that he did it to taste it,[15] though[16] he had not tasted the first bottle.[15] The prisoner ordered a servant to take away the basin, the dirty things, and the bottles, and put the bottles into her hands for that purpose; she put them down again on being directed by Lady Broughton to do so, but subsequently removed them on the peremptory order of the prisoner.[17] On the arrival of the apothecary the prisoner said the deceased had been out the preceding evening fishing, and had taken cold, but he said nothing of the draught which he had taken.[17] The prisoner had a still in his own room which he used for distilling roses;[18] and a few days after the death of Sir Theodosius he brought it full of wet lime to one of the servants to be cleaned.[19] The prisoner made several false and inconsistent statements to the servants as the cause of the young man's death;[20] and on the day of his death he wrote to Sir W. Wheeler, his guardian, to inform him of the event, but made no reference to its suddenness.[20] The coffin was soldered up

[15] Subsequent conduct influenced by a fact in issue and statements explanatory of conduct (section 8).

[16] This word is Mr. Wills's comment.

[17] Subsequent conduct and explanatory statements (section 8).

[18] Opportunity to distil laurel water, the poison said to have been used (section 7).

[19] Subsequent conduct (section 8).

[20] Admissions, 17, 18.

on the fourth day after the death.[21] Two days afterwards Sir W. Wheeler, in consequence of the rumours which had reached him of the manner of Sir Theodosius's death, and that suspicions were entertained that he had died from the effects of poison,[22] wrote a letter to the prisoner requesting that an examination might take place, and mentioning the gentlemen by whom he wished it to be conducted.[23] The prisoner accordingly sent for them, but did not exhibit Sir W. Wheeler's letter alluding to the suspicion that the deceased had been poisoned, nor did he mention to them that they were sent for at his request. Having been induced by the prisoner to suppose the case to be one of ordinary death,[24] and finding the body in an advanced state of putrefaction, the medical gentlemen declined to make the examination on the ground that it might be attended with personal danger. On the following day a medical man who had heard of their refusal to examine the body offered to do so, but the prisoner declined his offer on the ground that he had not been directed to send for him.[25] On the same day the prisoner wrote to Sir W. Wheeler a letter in which he stated that the medical men had fully satisfied the family, and endeavoured to account

[21] Introductory to what follows (section 9).

[22] Introductory to, and explanatory of, what follows (section 9). It should be observed that proof of the rumours and suspicions for the purpose of showing the truth of the matters rumoured and suspected would not be admissible. The fact that there were rumours and suspicions explains Sir W. Wheeler's letter.

[23] Statement to the prisoner and affecting his conduct (section 8, ex. 2).

[24] Subsequent conduct of prisoner (section 8) and Mr. Wills's comment on the conduct.

[25] Subsequent conduct (section 8). The fact that the first set of doctors refused explains the prisoner's conduct by showing that it had the effect of preventing examinations (section 7). The ground on which they refused tends to rebut this inference (section 9), but the second doctor's offer, and the prisoner's conduct thereon, tend to confirm it (section 9).

for the event by the ailment under which the deceased had been suffering; but he did not state that they had not made the examination.[26] Three or four days after, Sir W. Wheeler having been informed that the body had not been examined,[27] wrote to the prisoner insisting that it should be done,[28] which, however, he prevented by various disingenuous contrivances,[29] and the body was interred without examination.[30] In the meantime, the circumstances having become known to the coroner, he caused the body to be disinterred and examined on the eleventh day after death. Putrefaction was found to be far advanced, and the head was not opened, nor the bowels examined, and in other respects the examination was incomplete.[31] When Lady Broughton, in giving evidence before the coroner's inquest, related the circumstance of the prisoner having rinsed the bottles, he was observed to take hold of her sleeve and endeavour to check her, and he afterwards told her that she had no occasion to have mentioned that circumstance, but only to answer such questions as were put to her; and in a letter to the coroner and jury he endeavoured to impress them with the belief that the deceased had inadvertently poisoned himself with arsenic, which he had purchased to kill fish.[32] Upon the trial four medical men—three physicians and an apothecary—were examined on the part of the prosecution, and expressed a very decided opinion, mainly grounded upon the symptoms, the suddenness of the death, the *post-mortem* appearances, the smell of the draught

[26] Subsequent conduct (section 11) and admission (section 17).

[27] Introductory (section 9).

[28] Statement to the prisoner affecting his conduct (section 8, ex. 2.)

[29] Each contrivance and each circumstance which showed that it was disingenuous would come under the head of subsequent conduct (section 8).

[30] The burial was part of the transaction (section 6.) The absence of examination is explanatory of parts of the medical evidence. The whole is introductory to medical evidence (section 9).

[31] Introductory to opinions of experts (sections 9, 45, 46).

[32] Subsequent conduct (section 8) and admissions (section 17).

as observed by Lady Broughton, and the similar effects produced by experiments upon animals, that the deceased had been poisoned with laurel water;[33] one of them stating that on opening the body he had been affected with a biting acrimonious taste, like that which affected him in all the subsequent experiments with laurel water.[34] An eminent[35] surgeon and anatomist stated a positive opinion that the symptoms did not necessarily lead to the conclusion that the deceased had been poisoned, and that the appearances presented upon dissection explained nothing but putrefaction.[33] The prisoner was convicted and executed.

[33] Opinion of experts (section 45).

[34] This is a case of tasting a fact in issue, *viz.*, the laurel water present in the body. See definition of 'fact,' section 3.

[35] This was the famous John Hunter.

II.

Case of R. *v.* Belaney.*

A surgeon named Belaney was tried at the Central Criminal Court, August, 1844, before Mr. Baron Gurney, for the murder of his wife. They left their place of residence, at North Sunderland, on a journey of pleasure to London on the 1st of June (having a few days previously made mutual wills in each other's favour),[1] where on the 4th of that month they went into lodgings.[2] The deceased, who was advanced in pregnancy, was slightly indisposed after the journey; but not sufficiently so to prevent her going about with her husband.[3] On the 8th, being the Saturday morning after the arrival in town, the prisoner rang the bell for some hot water, a tumbler, and a spoon;[4] and he and his wife were heard conversing in their chamber about seven o'clock. About a quarter before eight the prisoner called the landlady up stairs, saying that his wife was very ill; and she found her lying motionless on the bed, with her eyes shut and her teeth closed, and foaming at the mouth. On being asked if she was subject to fits, the prisoner said she had had fits before, but none like this, and that she would not come out of it. On being pressed to send for a doctor, the prisoner said he was a doctor himself, and should have let blood before, but there was no pulse. On being further pressed to send for a doctor and his friends he

* Wills, on "Circumstantial Evidence," pp. 175-178.

[1] Motive (section 8).

[2] Introductory (section 9).

[3] State of things under which fact in issue happened (section 7).

[4] Preparation (section 8).

assented, adding that she would not come to; that this was an affection of the heart, and that her mother died in the same way nine months ago. The servant was accordingly sent to fetch two of the prisoner's friends, and on her return she and the prisoner put the patient's feet and hands in warm water, and applied a mustard plaster to her chest. A medical man was sent for, but before his arrival the patient had died.[5] There was a tumbler close to the head of the bed, about one-third full of something clear, but whiter than water; and there was also an empty tumbler on the other side of the table, and a paper of Epsom salts.[6] In reply to a question from a medical man whether the deceased had taken any medicine that morning, the prisoner stated that she had taken nothing but a little salts.[7] On the same morning the prisoner ordered a grave for interment on the following Monday.[8] In the meantime the contents of the stomach were examined, and found to contain prussic acid and Epsom salts. It was deposed that the symptoms were similar to those of death by prussic acid, but might be the result of any powerful sedative poison, and that the means resorted to by the prisoner were not likely to promote recovery; but that cold affusion, artificial respiration, and the application of brandy or ammonia (which in the shape of smelling salts is found in every house) and other stimulants were the appropriate remedies, and might probably have been effectual. No smell of prussic acid had been discovered in the room, though it has a very strong odour, but the window was open, and it was stated that the odour is soon dissipated by a current of air.[9] The prisoner

[5] The death and attendant circumstances are facts in issue and part of the transaction (sections 5, 26). The other facts are conduct (section 8) and admissions (sections 17, 18).

[6] State of things at death, or cause or effect of administration of poison (section 7).

[7] Admissions (sections 17, 18).

[8] Conduct (section 8).

[9] Effect of poisoning (section 7), opinions of experts (sections 45-46). The absence of the smell of prussic acid and the presence of the

had purchased prussic acid, as also acetate of morphine, on the preceding day, from a vender of medicines with whom he was intimate; but he had been in the habit of using these poisons under advice for a complaint in the stomach.[10] Two days after the fatal event the prisoner stated to the medical man, who had been called in and who had assisted in the examination of the body, that on the morning in question he was about to take some prussic acid; that on endeavouring to remove the stopper he had some difficulty, and used some force with the handle of a tooth-brush; that in consequence of breaking the neck of the bottle by the force, some of the acid was spilt; that he placed the remainder in the tumbler on the drawers at the end of the bed room, that he went into the front room to fetch a bottle wherein to place the acid, but instead of so doing began to write to his friends in the country, when in a few minutes he heard a scream from his wife's bed room, calling for cold water, and that the prussic acid was undoubtedly the cause of her death. Upon being asked what he had done with the bottle, the prisoner said he had destroyed it; and on being asked why he had not mentioned the circumstance before, he said he had not done so because he was so distressed and ashamed at the consequences of his negligence. To various persons in the north of England the prisoner wrote false and suspicious accounts of his wife's illness. In one of them, dated from the Euston Hotel on the 6th of June, he stated that his wife was unwell, and that two medical men attended her, and that in consequence he should give up an intended visit to Holland, and intimated his apprehension of a miscarriage. For these statements there was no foundation. At that time moreover he had removed from the Euston Hotel into lodgings, and on the same day he had made arrangements for leaving his wife in London, and

draft are respectively a fact suggesting the absence of prussic acid, and a fact rebutting that inference (section 9).

[10] Preparation (section 8) and fact rebutting inference from purchase of poison (section 9).

proceeding himself on his visit to Holland. In another letter, dated 8th of June, and posted after his wife's death, though it could not be determined whether it was written before or after, the prisoner stated that he had had his wife removed from the hotel to private lodgings, where she was dangerously ill and attended by two medical men, one of whom had pronounced her heart to be diseased; these representations were equally false. In another letter, dated the 9th of June, but not posted until the 10th, he stated the fact of his wife's death, but without any allusion to the cause; and in a subsequent letter he stated the reason for the suppression to be to conceal the shame and reproach of his negligence. The prisoner's statement to his landlady that his wife's mother had died from disease of the heart was also a falsehood, the prisoner having himself stated in writing to the registrar of burials that brain fever was the cause of death.[11] It was, however, proved that the prisoner was of a kind disposition, that he and his wife had lived upon affectionate terms and that he was extremely careless in his habits;[12] and no motive for so horrible a deed was clearly made out, though it was urged that it was the desire of obtaining her property by means of her testamentary disposition.[13] Upon the whole, though the case was to the last degree suspicious, it was certainly possible that an accident might have taken place in the way suggested; and the jury brought in a verdict of acquittal.

Remarks on cases of Donellan and Belaney.

The two cases of Donellan and Belaney are not merely curious in themselves, but throw light upon one of the most important of the points connected with judicial evidence, the point namely as to the amount of uncertainty which constitutes what can be called reasonable doubt. This I have already said is a question, not of calculation, but of prudence.

[11] All these are admissions (sections 17, 18), and conduct (section 3).
[12] Character (section 53).
[13] Motive (section 8).

The cases in question show that different tribunals at different times do not measure it in precisely the same way. In Donellan's case the jury did not think the possibility that Sir Theodosius Broughton might have died of a fit sufficiently great to constitute reasonable doubt as to his having been poisoned. In Belaney's case the jury thought that the possibility that the prisoner gave his wife the poison by accident did constitute a reasonable doubt as to his guilt. If the chances of the guilt and innocence of the two men could be numerically expressed, they would I think be as nearly as possible equal, and it might be said that both or that neither ought to have been convicted if it were not for the all-important principle that every case is independent of every other, and that no decision upon facts forms a precedent for any other decision. If two juries were to try the very same case, upon the same evidence and with the same summing up and the same arguments by counsel, they might very probably arrive at opposite conclusions, and yet it might be impossible to say that either of them was wrong. Of the moral qualifications for the office of a judge few are more important than the strength of mind which is capable of admitting the unpleasant truth that it is often necessary to act upon probabilities, and to run some risk of error. The cruelty of the old criminal law of Europe, and of England as well as of other countries produced many bad effects, one of which was that it intimidated those who had to put it in force. The saying that it is bettter that ten criminals should escape than that one innocent man should be convicted expresses this sentiment, which has I think been carried too far, and has done much to enervate the administration of justice.

III.

Case of R. *v.* Richardson.*

In the autumn of 1786 a young woman, who lived with her parents in a remote district in the stewartry of Kirkcudbright,[1] was one day left alone in the cottage,[2] her parents having gone out to the harvest-field.[3] On their return home a little after mid-day,[1] they found, their daughter murdered,[4] with her throat cut [5] in a most shocking manner.

The circumstances in which she was found, the character of the deceased, and the appearance of the wound, all concurred in excluding all supposition of suicide; [6] while the surgeons who examined the wound were satisfied that it had been inflicted by a sharp instrument, and by a person who must have held the weapon in his left hand.[7] Upon opening the body the deceased appeared to have been some months gone with child; [8]

* Wills, pp. 225-229. Mr. Wills observes, "This case is also concisely stated in the Memoirs of the Life of Sir Walter Scott, IV., p. 52, and it supplied one of the most striking incidents in Guy Mannering."

Introductory (section 9).

[2] Opportunity (section 7).

[3] Explanatory (section 9).

[4] Mr. Wills's comment. They found her with the throat cut, and Mr. Wills says she was murdered; but her murder was to them an inference, not a fact (section 3).

[5] Fact in issue (section 5).

[6] Suicide would be a relevant fact as being inconsistent with murder. The facts which exclude suicide are relevant as inconsistent with a relevant fact (section 11).

[7] Opinions of experts (section 45).

[8] State of things under which death happened (section 7). Motive section 8).

and on examining the ground about the cottage there were discovered the footsteps of a person who had seemingly been running hastily from the cottage by an indirect road through a quagmire or bog, in which there were stepping-stones.[9] It appeared, however, that the person in his haste and confusion had slipped his foot and stepped into the mire, by which he must have been wet nearly to the middle of the leg.[10] The prints of the footsteps were accurately measured, and an exact impression taken of them,[11] and it appeared that they were those of a person who must have worn shoes, the soles of which had been newly mended, and which, as is usual in that part of the country, had iron knobs or nails in them.[11] These were discovered also along the track of the footsteps, and at certain intervals drops of blood, and on a stile or small gateway near the cottage, and in the line of the footsteps some marks resembling those of a hand which had been bloody.[11] Not the slightest suspicion at this time attached to any particular person as the murderer, nor was it even suspected who might be the father of the child of which the girl was pregnant.[12] At the funeral a number of persons of both sexes attended,[13] and the steward-depute thought it the fittest opportunity of endeavouring, if possible, to discover the murderer conceiving rightly that, to avoid suspicion, whoever he was he would not on that occasion be absent.[12] With this view he called together, after the interment, the whole of the men who were present, being about sixty in number.[13] He caused

[9] Effects of fact in issue (section 7).

[10] This is so stated as to mix up inference and fact. Stripped of inference, the fact might have been stated thus,—'There were such marks in the bog as would have been produced if a person crossing the stepping-stones had slipped with one foot. The mud was of such a depth that a person so slipping would get wet to the middle of the leg.'

[11] Effects of fact in issue (section 7).

[12] Observation.

[13] Introductory (section 9).

the shoes of each of them to be taken off and measured, and one of the shoes was found to resemble pretty nearly the impression of the footsteps near to the cottage. The wearer of the shoe was the schoolmaster of the parish, which led to a suspicion that he must have been the father of the child, and had been guilty of the murder to save his character. On a closer examination of the shoe, it was discovered that it was pointed at the toe, whereas the impression of the footstep was round at that place.[14] The measurement of the rest went on, and after going through nearly the whole number, one at length was discovered which corresponded exactly with the impression in dimensions, shape of the foot, form of the sole, and the number and position of the nails.[15] William Richardson, the young man to whom the shoe belonged, on being asked where he was the day deceased was murdered, replied, seemingly without embarrassment, that he had been all that day employed at his master's work,[16] —a statement which his master and fellow-servants who were present confirmed.[17] This going so far to remove suspicion, a warrant of commitment was not then granted, but some circumstances occurring a few days afterwards having a tendency to excite it anew, the young man was apprehended and lodged in jail.[18] Upon

[14] Irrelevant.

[15] The making of the footmark was an effect of, or conduct subsequent to and affected by, a fact in issue (section 7). The measurement of the sixty.shoes, of which one only corresponded exactly with the mark, was a fact, or rather a set of facts, making highly probable the relevant fact that that shoe made that mark (section 11). The experiment itself is an application of the method of difference. This shoe would make the mark, and no other of a very large number would.

[16] This would be relevant against him, but not in his favour as an admission (sections 17, 18).

[17] The fact that his master and fellow-servants confirmed his statement is irrelevant. If they had testified afterwards to the fact itself, it would have been relevant.

[18] Irrelevant.

his examination[19] he acknowledged that he was left-handed;[20] and some scratches being observed on his cheek, he said he had got them when pulling nuts in a wood a few days before.[21] He still adhered to what he had said of his having been on the day of the murder employed constantly in his master's work;[22] but in the course of the inquiry it turned out that he had been absent from his work about half an hour, the time being distinctly ascertained, in the course of the forenoon of that day; that he called at a smith's shop under the pretence of wanting something which it did not appear that he had any occasion for; and that this smith's shop was in the way to the cottage of the deceased.[22] A young girl who was some hundred yards from the cottage, said that, about the time when the murder was committed (and which corresponded to the time when Richardson was absent from his fellow-servants), she saw a person exactly with his dress and appearance running hastily towards the cottage, but did not see him return, though he might have gone round by a small eminence which would intercept him from her view, and which was the very track where the footsteps had been traced.[23]

[19] By Scotch law, as well as by the Code of Criminal Procedure, a prisoner may be examined.

[20] The fact that he was left-handed would be a cause of a fact in issue, *viz.*, the peculiar way in which the fatal wound was given. The admission that he was left-handed would be relevant as proof of the fact by sections 17, 18.

[21] If it was suggested that the scratches were made in a struggle with the girl, they would be effects of a fact in issue (section 7), and the statement would be relevant as against the prisoner as an admission (section 17, 18).

[22] Opportunity (section 7). Admissions (sections 17, 18). The call at the shop was preparation by making evidence (section 8, illustration e).

[23] There is here a mixture of fact and inference; the girl could not know that a murder was committed at the time when it was committed. Probably she mentioned the time, and it corresponded with the time when Richardson was away. This would be preparation and opportunity (section 7). The existence of the small eminence explains her not seeing him return (section 9).

His fellow-servants now recollected that on the forenoon of that day they were employed with Richardson in driving their master's carts, and that, when passing by a wood which they named, he said that he must run to the smith's shop, and would be back in a short time. He then left his cart under their charge, and, having waited for him about half an hour, which one of the servants ascertained by having at the time looked at his watch, they remarked on his return that he had been absent a longer time than he said he would be, to which he replied that he had stopped in the wood to gather some nuts. They observed at the same time one of his stockings wet and soiled as if he had stepped in a puddle. He said he had stepped into a marsh, the name of which he mentioned, on which his fellow-servants remarked "that he must have been either mad or drunk if he stepped into that marsh, as there was a footpath which went along the side of it." It then appeared by comparing the time he was absent with the distance of the cottage from the place where he had left his fellow-servants that he might have gone there, committed the murder, and returned to them.[24] A search was then made for the stockings he had worn that day.[25] They were found concealed in the thatch of the apartment where he slept, and appeared to be much soiled, and to have some drops of blood on them.[26] The first he accounted for by saying, first, that his nose had been bleeding some days before; but it being observed that he wore other stockings on that day, he said he had assisted in bleeding a horse; but it was proved that he had not assisted, and had stood at such a distance that the blood could not have reached him.[27] On

[24] All these facts are either opportunity or preparation or subsequent or previous conduct or admissions (section 7, 8, 17).

[25] Introductory to next fact (section 91).

[26] The concealment is subsequent conduct (section 8). The state of the stockings is the effect of a fact in issue (section 7).

[27] The falsehoods are subsequent conduct (section 8), or admissions, (sections 17 & 18). The prisoner's allegation about the horse is an

examining the mud or sand upon the stockings, it appeared to correspond precisely with that of the mire or puddle adjoining the cottage, and which was of a very particular kind, none other of the same kind being found in that neighbourhood.[28] The shoemaker was then discovered who had mended his shoes a short time before, and he spoke distinctly to the shoes of the prisoner which were exhibited to him as having been those he had mended.[29] It then came out that Richardson had been acquainted with the deceased, who was considered in the country as of weak intellects, and had on one occasion been seen with her in a wood in circumstances that led to a suspicion that he had criminal intercourse with her, and, on being taunted with having such connection with one in her situation, he seemed much ashamed and greatly hurt.[30] It was proved further by the person who sat next him when his shoes were measuring, that he trembled much and seemed a good deal agitated, and that, in the interval between that time and his being apprehended, he had been advised to fly, but his answer was, "Where can I fly to?"[31]

On the other hand, evidence was brought to show that

---

allegation of a fact explaining the relevant fact, that there was blood on the stockings (section 9); and the fact proved about his distance from the horse is a fact rebutting the inference suggested thereby that the blood was the horse's (section 9).

[28] Effect of a fact in issue (section 7). The similarity of the sand on the stockings to the sand in the marsh was one of the effects of the slip, which was the effect of the murder.

[29] That the marks were made by the prisoner's shoe was relevant as an effect of facts in issue. That the shoes which made the marks were the prisoner's had been already proved by their being found on his feet. This further proof seems superfluous, unless it was suggested that they belonged to some one else.

[30] The opinion about her would be irrelevant. The fact that her intellect was weak would be part of the state of things under which the murder happened, and with what follows would show motive (sections 7, 8).

[31] Subsequent conduct (section 10). The weight of this is very slight.

about the time of the murder a boat's crew from Ireland had landed on that part of the coast near to the dwelling of the deceased;[32] and it was said that some of the crew might have committed the murder, though their motives for doing so it was difficult to explain, it not being alleged that robbery was their purpose, or that anything was missing from the cottages in the neighbourhood. The prisoner was convicted, confessed, and was hanged.

Remarks on Richardson's case.

This case illustrates the application of what Mr. Mill calls the method of agreement upon a scale which excludes the supposition of chance, thus:—

(1) The murderer had a motive,—Richardson had a motive.

(2) The murderer had an opportunity at a certain hour of a certain day in a certain place,—Richardson had an opportunity on that hour of that day at that place.

(3) The murderer was left-handed,—Richardson was left-handed.

(4) The murderer wore shoes which made certain marks,—Richardson wore shoes which made exactly similar marks.

(5) If Richardson was the murderer and wore stockings, they must have been soiled with a peculiar kind of sand,—he did wear stockings which were soiled with that kind of sand.

(6) If Richardson was the murderer, he would naturally conceal his stockings,—he did conceal his stockings.

(7) The murderer would probably get blood on his clothes,—Richardson got blood on his clothes.

(8) If Richardson was the murderer, he would probably tell lies about the blood,—he did tell lies about the blood.

(9) If Richardson was the murderer, he must have been at the place at the time in question,—a man very like him was seen running towards the place at the time.

(10) If Richardson was the murderer, he would probably

[32] Opportunity for the murder (section 7).

tell lies about his proceedings during the time when the murder was committed,—he told such lies.

Here are ten separate marks, five of which must have been found in the murderer, one of which must have been found on the murderer if he wore stockings, whilst others probably would be found in him.

All ten were found in Richardson. Four of them were so distinctive that they could hardly have met in more than one man. It is hardly imaginable that two left-handed men, wearing precisely similar shoes and closely resembling each other, should have put the same leg into the same hole of the same marsh at the same time, that one of them should have committed a murder, and that the other should have causelessly hidden the stockings which had got soiled in the marsh. Yet this would be the only possible supposition consistent with Richardson's innocence.

IV.

Case of R. *v.* Patch.*

A man named Patch had been received by Mr. Isaac Blight a ship-breaker, near Greenland Dock, into his service in the year 1803.[1] Mr. Bright having become embarrassed in his circumstances in July, 1805, entered into a deed of composition with his creditors; and in consequence of the failure of this arrangement, he made a colourable transfer of his property to the prisoner.[1] It was afterwards agreed between them that Mr. Blight was to retire nominally from the business, which the prisoner was to manage, and the former was to have two-thirds of the profits, and the prisoner the remaining third, for which he was to pay £1,250. Of this amount, £250 was paid in cash, and a draft was given for the remainder upon a person named Goom, which would become payable on the 16th of September, the prisoner representing that he had received the purchase-money of an estate and lent it to Goom.[2] On the 16th of September the prisoner represented to Mr. Blight's bankers that Goom could not take up the bill, and withdrew it, substituting his own draft upon Goom to fall due on the 20th September.[3] On the 19th of September the deceased went to visit his wife at Margate, and the prisoner accompanied him as far as Deptford,[4] and then went to London and represented to his bankers that

* Wills's Circumstantial Evidence.

[1] Introductory (section 9).

[2] Motive (section 8).

[3] Preparation (section 8).

[4] Introductory (section 9) but unimportant.

Goom would not be able to face his draft, but that he had obtained from him a note which satisfied him, and therefore they were not to present it.[5] The prisoner boarded in Mr. Blight's house, and the only other inmate was a female servant, whom the prisoner, about eight o'clock the same evening (the 19th), sent out to procure some oysters for his supper.[6] During her absence a gun or pistol ball was fired through the shutter of a parlour fronting the Thames, where the family, when at home, usually spent their evenings. It was low water, and the mud was so deep that any person attempting to escape in that direction must have been suffocated, and a man who was standing near the gate of the wharf, which was the only other mode of escape, heard the report, but saw no person.[7] From the manner in which the ball entered the shutter it was clear that it had been discharged by some person who was close to the shutter, and the river was so much below the level of the house, that the ball, if it had been fired from thence, must have reached a much higher part than that which it struck. The prisoner declined the offer of the neighbours to remain in the house with him that night.[8] On the following day he wrote to inform the deceased of the transaction, stating his hope that the shot had been accidental; that he knew of no person who had any animosity against him, that he wished

[5] Preparation (section 8).

[6] Explains what follows (section 9). Preparation (section 8).

[7] The suggestion was that Patch fired the shot himself in order to make evidence in his own favour. This would be preparation (section 8). Hence his firing the shot would be a relevant fact. The facts in the text are facts which, taken together, make it highly probable that he did so, as they show that he and no one else had the opportunity, and that it was done by some one (section 11).

The last fact illustrates the remarks made at pages 40, 41. The inference from the facts stated, assuming them to be true, is necessary; but, suppose that the "man standing near the gate" saw some one running, and for reasons of his own denied it, how could he be contradicted?

[8] Conduct (section 8).

to know for whom it was intended, and that he should be happy to hear from him, but much more so to see him.[9] Mr. Blight returned home on the 23rd September, having previously been to London to see his bankers on the subject of the £1,000 draft.[10] Upon getting home, the draft became the subject of conversation, and the deceased desired the prisoner to go to London, and not to return without the money.[11] Upon his return, the prisoner and the deceased spent the evening in the back parlour, a different one from that in which the family usually sat.[12] About eight o'clock the prisoner went from the parlour into the kitchen, and asked the servant for a candle[13], complaining that he was disordered.[14] The prisoner's way from the kitchen was through an outer door which fastened by a spring lock, and across a paved court in front of the house which was enclosed by palisades, and through a gate over a wharf in front of that court, on which there was the kind of soil peculiar to premises for breaking up ships, and then through a counting-house. All of these doors, as well as the door of the parlour, the prisoner left open, notwithstanding the state of alarm excited by the former shot. The servant heard the privy door slam, and almost at the same moment saw the flash of a pistol at the door of the parlour where the deceased was sitting, upon which she ran and shut the outer door and gate. The prisoner immediately afterwards rapped loudly at the door for admittance with his clothes in disorder. He evinced great apparent concern for Mr. Blight, who was mortally wounded, and died on the following day. From the state of tide, and from the testimony of various persons who were on the

[9] Preparation (section 8).

[10] Hardly relevant, except as introductory to what follows (section 9).

[11] Motive section 8).

[12] State of things under which facts in issue happened (section 7.)

[13] Preparation (section 8).

[14] Preparation (section 8).

outside of the premises, no person could have escaped from them.[15]

In consequence of this event Mrs. Blight returned home,[16] and the prisoner in answer to an inquiry about the draft which had made her husband so uneasy, told her that it was paid, and claimed the whole of the property as his own.[17] Suspicion soon fixed upon the prisoner,[18] and in his sleeping-room was found a pair of stockings rolled up like clean stockings, but with the feet plastered over with the sort of soil found on the wharf, and a ramrod was found in the privy.[19] The prisoner usually wore boots; but on the evening of the murder he wore shoes and stockings.[20] It was supposed that to prevent alarm to the deceased or the female servant, the murderer must have approached without his shoes, and afterwards gone on the wharf to throw away the pistol into the river.[21] All the prisoner's statements as to his pecuniary transactions with Goom and his right to draw upon him, and the payment of the bill, turned out to be false.[22] He attempted to tamper with the servant girl as to her evidence before the coroner, and urged her to keep to one account;[23] and before that officer he made several incon-

[15] These facts collectively are inconsistent with the firing of the shot by any one except Patch (section 11). They would also be relevant as being either facts in issue, or the state of things under which facts in issue happened (section 7), or as preparation or opportunity (sections 7 & 8, illustration *h.*).

[16] Introductory (section 9).

[17] Subsequent conduct influenced by a fact in issue (section 8).

[18] Irrelevant.

[19] Effect of fact in issue (section 7).

[20] State of things under which facts in issue happened (section 7).

[21] Fact and inference are mixed up in this statement; the facts are (1) that the state of things was such that the deceased and his servant would have heard the steps of a man with shoes on under the window; and (2) that a person who wished to throw anything into the Thames would have to go on to the wharf.

[22] Preparation (section 8).

[23] Subsequent conduct (section 8), and admissions (sections 17 & 18).

sistent statements as to his pecuniary transactions with the deceased, and equivocated much as to whether he wore boots or shoes on the evening of the murder, as well as to the ownership of the soiled stockings,[24] which, however, were clearly proved to be his, and for the soiled state of which he made no attempt to account.[24] The prisoner suggested the existence of malicious feelings in two persons with whom the deceased had been on ill terms,[25] but they had no motive[26] for doing him any injury; and it was clearly proved that upon both occasions of attack they were at a distance.[27]

Remarks on Patch's case.

Patch's case illustrates the method of difference, and the whole of it may be regarded as a very complete illustration of section 11. The general effect of the evidence is, that Patch had motive and opportunity for the murder, and that no one else, except himself, could have fired either the shot which caused the murdered man's death, or the shot which was intended to show that the murdered man had enemies who wished to murder him. The relevancy of the first shot arose from the suggestion that it was an act of preparation. The proof that it was fired by Patch consisted of independent facts, showing that it was fired, and that he, and no one else, could have fired it. The firing of the second shot by which the murder was committed was a fact in issue. The proof of it by a strange combination of circumstances was precisely similar in principle to the proof as to the first shot.

The case is also very remarkable as showing the way in which the chain of cause and effect links together facts of the most dissimilar kind; and this proves that it is impossible to draw a line between relevant and irrelevant facts otherwise than by enumerating as completely as possible the more common forms in which the relation of cause and effect displays itself. In Patch's case the firing of the first shot was

[24] Effect of fact in issue (section 7).
[25] Motive (section 8).

[26] *I.e.*, no special motive beyond general ill-will.

[27] Facts inconsistent with relevant fact (section 11).

* P. 34.

an act of preparation by way of what is called "making evidence," but the fact that Patch fired it appeared from a combination of circumstances which showed that he might, and that no one else could, have done so. It is easy to conceive that some one of the facts necessary to complete this proof might have had to be proved in the same way. For instance, part of the proof that Patch fired the shot consisted in the fact that no one left certain premises by a certain gate which was one of the suppositions necessary to be negatived in order to show that no one but Patch could have fired the shot. The proof given of this was the evidence of a man standing near, who said that at the time in question no one did pass through the gate in his presence, or could have done so unnoticed by him. Suppose that the proof had been that the gate had not been used for a long time; that spiders' webs had been spun all over the opening of the gate; that they were unbroken at night and remained unbroken in the morning after the shot; and that it was impossible that they should have been spun after the shot was fired and before the gate was examined. In that case the proof would have stood thus:—

Patch's preparations for the murder were relevant to the question whether he committed it. Patch's firing the first shot was one of his preparations for the murder. The facts inconsistent with his not having fired the shot were relevant to the question whether he fired it. The fact that a certain door was not opened between certain hours was one of the facts which, taken together, were inconsistent with his not having fired the shot. The fact that a spider's web was whole overnight and also in the morning was inconsistent with the door having been opened.

Inversely, the integrity of the spider's web was relevant to the opening of the door; the opening of the door was relevant to the firing of the first shot; the firing of the first shot was relevant to the firing of the second shot; and the firing of the second shot was a fact in issue; therefore the integrity of the spider's web was relevant to a fact in issue.

V.

Case of R. *v.* Palmer.[1]

On the 14th of May, 1856, William Palmer was tried at the Old Bailey, under powers conferred on the Court of Queen's Bench by 19 Vic., c. 16, for the murder of John Parsons Cook at Rugeley, in Staffordshire. The trial lasted twelve days, and ended on the 27th May, when the prisoner was convicted, and received sentence of death, on which he was afterwards executed at Stafford.

Palmer was a general medical practitioner at Rugeley, much engaged in sporting transactions. Cook, his intimate friend, was also a sporting man; and after attending Shrewsbury races with him on the 13th November, 1855, returned in his company to Rugeley, and died at the Talbot Arms Hotel, at that place, soon after midnight, on the 21st November, 1855, under circumstances which raised a suspicion that he had been poisoned by Palmer. The case against Palmer was that he had a strong motive to murder his friend, and that his conduct before, at the time of, and after his death, coupled with the circumstances of the death itself, left no reasonable doubt that he did murder him by poisoning him with antimony and strychnine, administered on various occasions—the antimony probably being used as a preparation for the strychnine.

The evidence stood as follows:—At the time of Cook's death, Palmer was involved in bill transactions which appear to have begun in the year 1853. His wife died in September,

[1] Reprinted from my "General View of the Criminal Law of England," p. 357.

1854, and on her death he received £13,000 on policies on her life, nearly the whole of which was applied to the discharge of his liabilities.[2] In the course of the year 1855 he raised other large sums, amounting in all to £13,500, on what purpörted to be acceptances of his mother's. The bills were renewed from time to time at enormous interest (usually sixty per cent. per annum) by a money-lender named Pratt, who, at the time of Cook's death, held eight bills—four on his own account and four on account of his client; two already overdue, and six others falling due—some in November and others in January. About £1,000 had been paid off in the course of the year, so that the total amount then due, or shortly to fall due to Pratt, was £12,500. The only means which Palmer had by which these bills could be provided for was a policy on the life of his brother, Walter Palmer, for £13,000. Walter Palmer died in August, 1855,[3] and William Palmer had instructed Pratt to recover the amount from the insurance office, but the office refused to pay. In consequence of this difficulty, Pratt earnestly pressed Palmer to pay something in order to keep down the interest or diminish the principal due on the bills. He issued writs against him and his mother on the 6th November, and informed him in substance that they would be served at once, unless he would pay something on account. Shortly before the Shrewsbury races he had accordingly paid three sums, amounting in all to £800, of which £600 went in reduction of the principal, and £200 was deducted for interest. It was understood that more money was to be raised as early as possible.

Besides the money due to Pratt, Mr. Wright of Birmingham held bills for £10,400. Part of these, amounting to £6,500, purported to be accepted by Mrs. Palmer, part were collaterally secured by a bill of sale of the whole of William Palmer's property. These bills would fall due on the first or second week of November. Mr. Padwick also held a bill of

[2] A bill was found against him for her murder.

[3] A bill was found against Palmer for his murder.

the same kind for £2,000, on which £1,000 remained unpaid, and which was twelve months overdue on the 6th of October, 1855. Palmer, on the 12th November, had given Espin a cheque antedated on the 28th November, for the other £1,000. Mrs. Sarah Palmer's acceptance was on nearly all these bills, and in every instance was forged.

The result is, that about the time of the Shrewsbury races, Palmer was being pressed for payment on forged acceptances to the amount of nearly £20,000, and that his only resources were a certain amount of personal property, over which Wright held a bill of sale, and a policy for £13,000, the payment of which was refused by the office. Should he succeed in obtaining payment, he might no doubt struggle through his difficulties, but there still remained the £1,000 antedated cheque given to Espin, which it was necessary to provide for at once by some means or other. That he had no funds of his own was proved by the fact that his balance at the bank on the 19th November was £9 6s. and that he had to borrow £25 of a farmer named Wallbank, to go to Shrewsbury races. It follows that he was under the most pressing necessity to obtain a considerable sum of money, as even a short delay in obtaining it might involve him not only in insolvency, but in a prosecution for uttering forged acceptances.

Besides the embarrassment arising from the bills in the hands of Pratt, Wright, and Padwick, Palmer was involved in a transaction with Cook, which had a bearing on the rest of the case. Cook and he were parties to a bill for £500 which Pratt had discounted, giving £365 in cash, and a wine warrant for £65, and charging £60 for discount and expenses. He also required an asignment of two racehorses of Cook's —Pole-star and Sirius—as a collateral security. By Palmer's request the £365, in the shape of a cheque payable to Cook's order, and the wine warrant, were sent by post to Palmer at Doncaster. Palmer wrote Cook's endorsement on the cheque, and paid the amount to his own credit at the bank at Rugeley. On the part of the prosecution it was said that this transaction afforded a reason why Palmer should desire to be rid of Cook, inasmuch as it amounted to a forgery by which Cook was defrauded of £375. It appeared, however, on the other side, that there were £300 worth of notes relating to some other transaction, in the letter which enclosed the cheque; and as it did not appear that Cook had complained of getting no consideration for his acceptance, it was suggested that he had authorized Palmer to write his name on the back of the cheque, and had taken the notes himself. This arrangement seems not improbable, as it would otherwise be hard to explain why Cook acquiesced in receiving nothing for his acceptance, and there was evidence that he meant to provide for the bill when it became due. It also appeared late in the case that there was another bill for £500, in which Cook and Palmer were jointly interested.[1]

Such was Palmer's position when he went to Shrewsbury races, on Monday, the 12th November, 1855. Cook was there also; and on Tuesday, the 13th, his mare Pole-star won the Shrewsbury Handicap, by which he became entitled to the stakes, worth about £380, and bets to the amount of nearly £2,000. Of these bets he received £700 or £800 on the course at Shrewsbury. The rest was to be paid at Tattersall's on the following Monday, the 19th November.[1] After the race Cook invited some of his friends to dinner at the Raven Hotel, and on that occasion and on the following day he was both sober and well.[2] On the Wednesday night a man named Ishmael Fisher came into the sitting-room, which Palmer shared with Cook, and found them in company with some other men drinking brandy and water. Cook complained that the brandy "burned his throat dreadfully," and put down his glass with a small quantity remaining in it. Palmer drank up what was left, and, handing the glass to Read, asked him if he thought there was anything in it to

[1] All these facts go to show motive (section 8).

[2] State of things under which the following facts occurred (section 7).

which Read replied, "What's the use of handing me the glass when it's empty?" Cook shortly afterwards left the room, called out Fisher, and told him that he had been very sick, and, "he thought that damned Palmer had dosed him." He also handed over to Fisher £700 or £800 in notes to keep for him.[6] He then became sick again, and was ill all night, and had to be attended by a doctor. He told the doctor, Mr. Gibson, that he thought he had been poisoned, and he was treated on that supposition.[7] Next day Palmer told Fisher that Cook had said that he (Palmer) had been putting something into his brandy. He added that he did not play such tricks with people, and that Cook had been drunk the night before—which appeared not to be the case.[8] Fisher did not expressly say that he returned the money to Cook, but from the course of the evidence it seems that he did,[9] for Cook asked him to pay Pratt £200 at once, and to repay himself on the following Monday out of the bets which he would receive on Cook's account at the settling at Tattersall's.

About half-past ten on the Wednesday, and apparently shortly before Cook drank the brandy and water which he complained of, Palmer was seen by a Mrs. Brooks in the passage looking at a glass lamp through a tumbler which contained some clear fluid like water, and which he was shaking and turning in his hand. There appears, however, to have been no secrecy in this, as he spoke to Mrs. Brooks and continued to hold and shake the tumbler as he did so.[10]

[6] Conduct of person against whom offence was committed, and statement explanatory of such conduct (section 8; exp. 1).

[7] The administration of antimony by Palmer would be a fact in issue, as being one of a set of acts of poisoning which finally caused Cook's death. Cook's feelings were relevant as the effect of his being poisoned (section 7); and his statement as to them was relevant under section 14 as a statement showing, the existence of a relevant bodily feeling.

[8] Admission (sections 17, 18).

[9] Motive (section 8).

[10] Preparation (section 8).

George Myatt was called to contradict this for the prisoner. He said that he was in the room when Palmer and Cook came in ; that Cook made a remark about the brandy, though he gave a different version of it from Fisher and Read ; that he did not see anything put in it, and that if anything had been put in it he should have seen. He also swore that Palmer never left the room from the time he came in till Cook went to bed. He also put the time later than Fisher and Read.[11] All this, however, came to very little. It was the sort of difference which always arises in the details of evidence. As Myatt was a frend of Palmer's, he probably remembered the matter (perhaps honestly enough) in a way more favourable to him than the other witnesses.

It appeared from the evidence of Mrs. Brooks, and also from that of a man named Herring, that other persons besides Cook were taken ill at Shrewsbury, on the evening in question, with similar symptoms. Mrs. Brooks said, "We made an observation we thought the water might have been poisoned in Shrewsbury." Palmer himself vomited on his way back to Rugeley according to Myatt.[12]

The evidence as to what passed at Shrewsbury clearly proves that Palmer, being then in great want of money, Cook was to his knowledge in possession of £700 or £800 in bank-notes, and was also entitled to receive on the following Monday about £1,400 more. It also shows that Palmer may have given him a dose of antimony, though the weight of the evidence to this effect is weakened by the proof that diarrhœa and vomiting were prevalent in Shrewsbury at the time, It is, however, important in connection with subsequent events.

On Thursday, November 15th, Palmer and Cook returned together to Rugeley, which they reached about ten at night. Cook went to the Talbot Arms, and Palmer to his own house

[11] Evidence against last fact (section 5).

[12] Facts rebutting inference suggested by preceding fact (section 9).

immediately opposite. Cook still complained of being unwell. On the Friday he dined with Palmer, in company with an attorney, Mr. Jeremiah Smith, and returned perfectly sober about ten in the evening.[13] At eight on the following morning (November 17th) Palmer came over, and ordered a cup of coffee for him. The coffee was given to Cook by Mills the chambermaid, in Palmer's presence. When she next went to his room, an hour or two afterwards, it had been vomited.[14] In the course of the day, and apparently about the middle of the day, Palmer sent a charwoman, named Rowley, to get some broth for Cook at an inn called the Albion. She brought it to Palmer's house, put it by the fire to warm, and left the room. Soon after Palmer brought it out, poured it into a cup, and sent it to the Talbot Arms with a message that it came from Mr. Jeremiah Smith. The broth was given to Cook, who at first refused to take it; Palmer, however, came in, and said he must have it. The chambermaid brought back the broth which she had taken downstairs, and left it in the room. It also was thrown up.[14] In the course of the afternoon Palmer called in Mr. Bamford, a surgeon eighty years of age, to see Cook, and told him that when Cook dined at his (Palmer's) house he had taken too much champagne.[15] Mr. Bamford, however, found no bilious symptoms about him, and he said he had only drunk two glasses.[16] On the Saturday night Mr. Jeremiah Smith slept in Cook's room, as he was still ill. On the Sunday, between twelve and one, Palmer sent over his gardener, Hawley, with some more

[13] Introductory to what follows (section 9), and shows state of things under which following facts occurred (section 7).

[14] Fact in issue and its effect, as this was an act of poisoning (section 5).

[15] Conduct and statements explaining conduct (section 8).

[16] Rebuts inference in Palmer's favour, suggested by preceding fact and explains the object of his conduct by showing that his statement was false (section 9). Cook's statement relates to his state of body (section 14).

broth for Cook.[17] Elizabeth Mills, the servant at the Talbot Arms, tasted it, taking two or three spoonfuls. She became exceedingly sick about half an hour afterwards, and vomited till five o'clock in the afternoon. She was so ill that she had to go to bed. This broth was also taken to Cook, and the cup afterwards returned to Palmer. It appears to have been taken and vomited, though the evidence is not quite explicit on that point.[18] By the Sunday's post Palmer wrote to Mr. Jones, an apothecary, and Cook's most intimate friend, to come and see him. He said that Cook was "confined to his bed with a severe bilious attack, combined with diarrhœa." The servant Mills said there was no diarrhœa.[19] It was observed on the part of the defence that this letter was strong proof of innocence. The prosecution suggested that it was "part of a deep design, and was meant to make evidence in the prisoner's favour." The fair conclusion seems be to that it was an ambiguous act which ought to weigh neither way, though the falsehood about Cook's symptoms is suspicious as far as it goes.

On the night between Sunday and Monday Cook had some sort of attack. When the servant Mills went into his room on the Monday he said, "I was just mad for two minutes." She said, "Why did you not ring the bell?" He said, "I thought that you would be all fast asleep, and not hear it." He also said he was disturbed by a quarrel in the street. It might have waked and disturbed him, but he was not sure. This incident was not mentioned at first by Barnes and Mills, but was brought out on their being recalled at the request of the prisoner's counsel. It was considered important for the defence, as proving that Cook had had an attack of some kind before it was suggested that any strychnine was administered; and the principal medical

[17] Fact in issue—administration of poison (section 5).

[18] Effects of facts in issue (section 7).

[19] Conduct (section 8), and explanation of it (section 9).

witness for the defence, Mr. Nunneley, referred to it with this view.[20]

On the Monday, about a quarter-past or half-past seven, Palmer again visited Cook; but as he was in London about half-past two, he must have gone to town by an early train. During the whole of the Monday Cook was much better. He dressed himself, saw a jockey and his trainer, and the sickness ceased.[21]

In the meantime Palmer was in London. He met by appointment a man named Herring, who was connected with the turf. Palmer told him he wished to settle Cook's account and read to him from a list, which Herring copied as Palmer read it, the particulars of the bets which he was to receive. They amounted to £984 clear. Of this sum Palmer instructed Herring to pay £450 to Pratt and £350 to Padwick. The nature of the debt to Padwick was not proved in evidence, as Padwick himself was not called. Palmer told Herring the £450 was to settle the bill for which Cook had assigned his horses. He wrote Pratt on the same day a letter in these words :—" Dear Sir,—you will place the £50 I have just paid you, and the £450 you will receive from Mr. Herring, together £500, and the £200 you received on Saturday " (from Fisher) " towards payment of my mother's acceptance for £2,000 due 25th October.[22]

Herring received upwards of £800, and paid part of it away according to Palmer's directions. Pratt gave Palmer credit for the £450 ; but the £350 was not paid to Padwick, according to Palmer's directions, as part was retained by Mr. Herring for some debts due from Cook to him, and Herring received less than he expected. In his reply the Attorney-General said that the £350 intended to be paid to Padwick was on account of a bet, and suggested that the motive was to keep

[20] Fact tending to rebut inference from previous facts (section 9).

[21] Supports the inference suggested by the previous fact that Palmer's doses caused Cook's illness (section 9).

[22] Conduct and statement explanatory thereof (section 8, ex. 2).

Padwick quiet as to the ante dated cheque for £1,000 given to Espin on Padwick's account. There was no evidence of this, and it is not of much importance. It was clearly intended to be paid to Padwick on account, not of Cook (except possibly as to a small part), but of Palmer. Palmer thus disposed, or attempted to dispose, in the course of Monday, Nov. 19th, of the whole of Cook's winnings for his own advantage.[23]

This is a convenient place to mention the final result of the transaction relating to the bill for £500, in which Cook and Palmer were jointly interested. On the Friday when Cook and Palmer dined together (Nov. 16), Cook wrote to Fisher (his agent) in these words:—" It is of very great im-" portance to both Palmer and myself that a sum of £500 " should be paid to a Mr. Pratt, of 5, Queen Street, Mayfair; " 300*l. has been sent up to-night,* and if you would be kind " enough to pay the other £200 to-morrow, on the receipt of " this, you will greatly oblige me. I will settle it on Monday " at Tattersall's." Fisher did pay the £200, expecting, as he said, to settle Cook's account on the Monday, and repay himself. On the Saturday, Nov. 17th (the day after the date of the letter), " a person," said Pratt, " whose name I did not " know, called on me with a cheque, and paid me 300*l.* on " account of *the prisoner;* that" (apparently the cheque, not the 300*l.*) " was a cheque of Mr. Fisher's." When Pratt heard of Cook's death he wrote to Palmer, saying, " The death of " Mr. Cook will now compel you to look about as to the payment of the bill for £500 due the 2nd of December." [24]

Great use was made of these letters by the defence. It was argued that they proved that Cook was helping Palmer, and was eager to relieve him from the pressure put on him by Pratt; that in consequence of this he not only took up the £500 bill, but authorized Palmer to apply the £800 to similar

[23] All this is Palmer's conduct, and is explanatory of it (section 7, 9).

[24] Motive for not poisoning Cook (section 8).

purposes, and to get the amount settled by Herring, instead of Fisher, so that Fisher might not stop out of it the £200 which he had advanced to Pratt. It was asked how it could be Palmer's interest, on this supposition, that Cook should die, especially as the first consequence of his death was Pratt's application for the money due on the £500 bill.

These arguments were, no doubt, plausible; and the fact that Cook's death compelled Pratt to look to Palmer for the payment of the £500 lends them weight; but it may be asked, on the other hand, why should Cook give away the whole of his winnings to Palmer? Why should Cook allow Palmer to appropriate to the diminution of his own liabilities the £200 which Fisher had advanced to the credit of the bill on which both were liable? Why should he join with Palmer in a plan for defrauding Fisher of his security for this advance? No answer to any of these questions was suggested. As to the £300, Cook's letter to Fisher says, "£300 *has been* sent up this evening." There was evidence that Pratt never received it, for he applied to Palmer for the money on Cook's death. Moreover Pratt said that on the Saturday he did receive £300 *on account of Palmer*, which he placed to the account of the forged acceptance for £2,000. Where did Palmer get the money? The suggestion of the prosecution was that Cook gave it him to pay to Pratt on account of their joint bill, and that he paid it on his own account. This was probably the true view of the case. The observation that Pratt, on hearing of Cook's death, applied to Palmer to pay the £500 bill, is met by the reflection that that bill was genuine, and collaterally secured by the assignment of the racehorses, and that the other bill bore a forged acceptance, and must be satisfied at all hazards. The result is that on the Monday evening Palmer had the most imperious interest in Cook's death, for he had robbed him of all he had in the world, except the equity of redemption in his two horses.

On Monday evening (Nov. 19th) Palmer returned to Rugeley, and went to the shop of Mr. Salt, a surgeon there, about nine p.m. He saw Newton, Salt's assistant, and asked him for three grains of strychnine, which were accordingly given him.[25] Newton never mentioned this transaction till a day or two before his examination as a witness in London, though he was examined on the inquest. He explained this by saying that there had been a quarrel between Palmer and Salt, his (Newton's) master, and that he thought Salt would be displeased with him for having given Palmer anything. No doubt the concealment was improper, but nothing appeared on cross-examination to suggest that the witness was willfully perjured.

Cook had been much better throughout Monday, and on Monday evening Mr. Bamford, who was attending him, brought some pills for him, which he left at the hotel. They contained neither antimony nor strychnine. They were taken up in the box in which they came to Cook's room by the chambermaid, and were left there on the dressing-table about eight o'clock. Palmer came (according to Barnes, the waitress) between eight and nine, and Mills said she saw him sitting by the fire between nine and ten.[26]

If this evidence were believed he would have had an opportunity of substituting poisoned pills for those sent by Mr. Bamford just after he had, according to Newton, procured strychnine. The evidence, however, was contradicted by a witness called for the prisoner, Jeremiah Smith the attorney. He said that on the Monday evening, about ten minutes past ten, he saw Palmer coming in a car from the directon of Stafford; that they then went up to Cook's room together, stayed two or three minutes, and went with Smith to the house of old Mrs. Palmer, his mother. Cook said "Bamford sent him some pills, and he had taken them, and Palmer was late, intimating that he should not have taken them if he had thought Palmer would have called in before." If this evidence were believed it would of course have proved that Cook took the pills which

[25] Preparation (section 8).

[26] Opportunity. The rest is introductory (section 7, 9).

Bamford sent as he sent them.[27] Smith, however, was cross-examined by the Attorney-General at great length. He admitted with the greatest reluctance that he had witnessed the assignment of a policy for £13,000 by Walter to William Palmer; that he wrote to an office to effect an insurance for £10,000 on the life of Bates, who was Palmer's groom, at £1 a week; that he tried, after Walter Palmer's death, to get his widow to give up her claim on the policy; that he was applied to to attest other proposals for insurances on Walter Palmer's life for similar amounts; and that he had got a cheque for £5 for attesting the assignment.[28]

Lord Campbell said of this witness in summing up, "Can you believe a man who so disgraces himself in the witness-box? It is for you to say what faith you can place in a witness, who, by his own admission, engaged in such fraudulent proceedings."

It is curious that though the credit of this witness was so much shaken in cross-examination, and though he was contradicted both by Mills and Newton, he must have been right and they wrong as to the time when Palmer came down to Rugeley that evening. Mr. Matthews, the inspector of police at the Euston station, proved that the only train by which Palmer could have left London after half-past two (when he met Herring) started at five, and reached Stafford on the night in question at a quarter to nine. It is about ten miles from Stafford to Rugeley, so that he could not have got across by the road in much less than an hour;[29] yet Newton said he saw him "about nine," and Mills saw him "between nine and ten." Nothing, however, is more difficult than to speak accurately to time; on the other hand, if Smith spoke the truth Newton

[27] Evidence against the existence of the fact last mentioned (section 5).

[28] This cross-examination tended to test the veracity of the witness and to test his credit (section 146).

[29] Facts inconsistent with a relevant fact (section 11), and fixing he time of the occurrence of a relevant fact (section 9).

could not have seen him at all that night, and Mills, if at all, must have seen him for a moment only in Smith's company. Mills never mentioned Smith, and Smith would not venture to swear that she or any one else saw him at the Talbot Arms. It was a suspicious circumstance that Serjeant Shee did not open Smith's evidence to the jury. An opportunity for perjury was afforded by the mistake made by the witnesses as to the time, which the defence were able to prove by the evidence of the police inspector. If Smith were disposed to tell an untruth, the knowledge of this fact would enable him to do so with an appearance of plausibility.

Whatever view is taken as to the effect of this evidence it was clearly proved that about the middle of the night between Monday and Tuesday Cook had a violent attack of some sort. About twelve, or a little before, his bell rang; he screamed violently. When Mills, the servant, came in he was sitting up in bed, and asked that Palmer might be fetched at once. He was beating the bedclothes; he said he should suffocate if he lay down. His head and neck and his whole body jumped and jerked. He had great difficulty in breathing, and his eyes protruded. His hand was stiff, and he asked to have it rubbed. Palmer came in, and gave him a draught and some pills. He snapped at the glass, and got both it and the spoon between his teeth. He had also great difficulty in swallowing the pills. After this he got more easy, and Palmer stayed by him some time, sleeping in an easy chair.[27]

Great efforts were made in cross-examination to shake the evidence of Mills by showing that she had altered the evidence which she gave before the coroner, so as to make her description of the symptoms tally with those of poisoning by strychnine, and also by showing that she had been drilled as to the evidence which she was to give by persons connected with the prosecution. She denied most of the suggestions

30 Effect of fact in issue, *viz.*, the administration of poison (section 7).

conveyed by the questions asked her, and explained others.[31] As to the differences between her evidence before the coroner and at the trial, a witness (Mr. Gardner, an attorney) was called to show that the depositions were not properly taken at the inquest.[32]

On the following day, Tuesday, the 20th, Cook was a good deal better. In the middle of the day he sent the boots to ask Palmer if he might have a cup of coffee. Palmer said he might, and came over, tasted a cup made by the servant, and took it from her hands to give it to Cook. This coffee was afterwards thrown up.[33]

A little before or after this, the exact hour is not important, Palmer went to the shop of Hawkins, a druggist at Rugeley, and was there served by his apprentice Roberts with two drachms of prussic acid, six grains of strychnine, and two drachms of Batley's sedative.[34] Whilst he was making the purchase, Newton, from whom he had obtained the other strychnine the night before, came in; Palmer took him to the door, saying he wished to speak to him; and when he was there asked him a quesion about the farm of a Mr. Edwin Salt—a matter with which he had nothing at all to do. Whilst they were there a third person came up and spoke to Newton, on which Palmer went back into Hawkins' shop and took away the things, Newton not seeing what he took. The obvious suggestion upon this is that Palmer wanted to prevent Newton from seeing what he was about. No attempt

[31] Former statements inconsistent with evidence (section 155).

[32] The depositions before the coroner would be a proper mode of proof as being a record of a relevant fact made by a public servant in the discharge of his official duty (section 35), and any document purporting to be such a deposition would on production be presumed to be genuine, and the evidence would be presumed to be duly taken (sections 79 and 80), but this might be rebutted (section 8), definition of 'shall presume.'

[33] Part of the transaction of poisoning (section 8).

[34] Preparation (section 8).

even was made to shake, or in any way discredit, Roberts the apprentice.[32]

At about four p.m. Mr. Jones, the friend to whom Palmer had written, arrived from Lutterworth.[33] He examined Cook in Palmer's presence, and remarked that he had not the tongue of a bilious patient; to which Palmer replied, "You should have seen it before." Cook appeared to be better during the Tuesday, and was in good spirits.[34] At about seven p.m. Mr. Bamford came in, and Cook told him in Palmer's presence that he objected to the pills, as they had made him ill the night before. The three medical men then had a private consultation. Palmer proposed that Bamford should make up the pills as on the night before, and that Jones should not tell Cook what they were made of, as he objected to the morphine which they contained. Bamford agreed, and Palmer went up to his house with him and got the pills, and was present whilst they were made up, put into a pill-box, and directed. He took them away with him between seven and eight.[35] Cook was well and comfortable all the evening; he had no bilious symptoms, no vomiting, and no diarrhœa.[34]

Towards eleven Palmer came with a box of pills directed in Bamford's hand. He called Jones's attention to the goodness of the handwriting for a man of eighty.[36] It was suggested by the prosecution that the reason for this was to impress Jones with the fact that the pills had been made up by Bamford. With reference to Smith's evidence it is remarkable that Bamford on the second night sent the pills, not "between nine and ten," but at eleven. Palmer pressed Cook to take the pills, which at first he refused to do, as they had made him so ill the night before. At last he did so, and immediately afterwards vomited. Jones and Palmer both examined to see whether the pills had been thrown up, and they found that

[32] Conduct (section 8). [33] Introductory (section 9).

[34] State of things under which Cook was poisoned (section 7).

[35] Preparation (section 8).

[36] Conduct and statements (section 8, ex. 2).

they had not. This was about eleven. Jones then had his supper, and went to bed in Cook's room about twelve. When he had been in bed a short time, perhaps ten minutes, Cook started up and called out, "Doctor, get up; I am going to be ill; ring the bell for Mr. Palmer." He also said, "Rub my neck." The back of his neck was stiff and hard. Mills ran across the road to Palmer's and rang the bell. Palmer immediately came to the bedroom window and said he would come at once. Two minutes afterwards he was in Cook's room, and said he had never dressed so quick in his life. He was dressed as usual. The suggestion upon this was that he had been sitting up expecting to be called.[37]

By the time of Palmer's arrival Cook was very ill. Jones, Elizabeth Mills, and Palmer were in the room, and Barnes stood at the door. The muscles of his neck were stiff; he screamed loudly. Palmer gave him what he said were two ammonia pills. Immediately afterwards—too soon for the pills to have any effect—he was dreadfully convulsed. He said, when he began to be convulsed, "Raise me up, or I shall be suffocated." Palmer and Jones tried to do so; but could not, as the limbs were rigid. He then asked to be turned over, which was done. His heart began to beat weakly. Jones asked Palmer to get some ammonia to try to stimulate it. He fetched a bottle, and was absent about a minute for that purpose. When he came back Cook was almost dead, and he died in a few minutes, quite quietly. The whole attack lasted about ten minutes. The body was twisted back into the shape of a bow, and would have rested on the head and heels, had it been laid on its back. When the body was laid out, it was very stiff. The arms could not be kept down by the sides till they were tied behind the back with tape. The feet also had to be tied, and the fingers of one hand were very stiff, the hand being clenched. This was about one a.m., half or three quarters of an hour after the death.[38]

[37] Fact in issue (section 15). Conduct (section 8).

[38] Cook's death, in all its detail, was a fact in issue (section 5).

As soon as Cook was dead, Jones went out to speak to the housekeeper, leaving Palmer alone with the body. When Jones left the room he sent the servant Mills in, and she saw Palmer searching the pockets of Cook's coat and searching also under the pillow and bolster. Jones shortly afterwards returned, and Palmer told him that as Cook's nearest friend, he (Jones) ought to take possession of his property. He accordingly took possession of his watch and purse, containing five sovereigns and five shillings. He found no other money. Palmer said, "Mr. Cook's death is a bad thing for me, as I am responsible for £3,000 or £4,000; and I hope Mr. Cook's friends will not let me lose it. If they do not assist me, all my horses will be seized." The betting-book was mentioned. Palmer said, "It will be no use to any one," and added that it would probably be found.[39]

On Wednesday, the 21st inst., Mr. Wetherby, the London racing agent, who kept a sort of bank for sporting men, received from Palmer a letter enclosing a cheque for £350 against the amount of the Shrewsbury stakes (£381), which Wetherby was to receive for him. This cheque had been drawn on the Tuesday, about seven o'clock in the evening, under peculiar circumstances. Palmer sent for Mr. Cheshire, the postmaster at Rugeley, telling him to bring a receipt stamp, and when he arrived asked him to write out, from a copy which he produced, a cheque by Cook on Wetherby. He said it was for money which Cook owed him, and that he was going to take it over for Cook to sign. Cheshire wrote out the body of the cheque, and Palmer took it away. When Mr. Wetherby received the cheque, the stakes had not been paid to Cook's credit. He accordingly returned the cheque to Palmer, to whom the prosecution gave notice to produce it at the trial.[40] It was called for, but not produced.[41] This

[39] Conduct (section 8).

[40] Conduct (section 8).

[41] See section 66 as to notice to produce.

was one of the strongest facts against Palmer in the whole of the case. If he had produced the cheque, and if it had appeared to have been really signed by Cook, it would have shown that Cook, for some reason or other, had made over his stakes to Palmer, and this would have destroyed the strong presumption arising from Palmer's appropriation of the bets to his own purposes. In fact, it would have greatly weakened and almost upset the case as to the motive. On the other hand, the non-production of the cheque amounted to an admission that it was a forgery; and if that were so, Palmer was forging his friend's name for the purpose of stealing his stakes at the time when to all outward appearance there was every prospect of his speedy recovery which must result in the detection of the fraud. If he knew that Cook would die that night, this was natural. On any other supposition it was inconceivable rashness.[42]

Either on Thursday, 22nd, or Friday, 23rd, Palmer sent for Cheshire again, and produced a paper which he said Cook had given to him some days before. The paper purported to be an acknowledgment that certain bills—the particulars of which were stated—were all for Cook's benefit, and not for Palmer's. The amount was considerable, as at least one item was for £1,000, and another for £500. This document purported to be signed by Cook, and Palmer wished Cheshire to attest Cook's execution of it, which he refused to do. This document was called for at the trial, and not produced. The same observations apply to it as to the cheque.[40, 41, 42]

Evidence was further given to show that Palmer, who, shortly before, had but £9 6s. at the bank, and had borrowed £25 to go to Shrewsbury, paid away large sums of money soon after Cook's death. He paid Pratt £100 on the 24th; he paid a farmer named Spilsbury £46 2s. with a Bank of England note for £50 on the 22nd; and Bown, a draper, a sum of £60 or thereabouts in two £50 notes, on the 20th,[43]

[42] As to these inferences see section 114, illust. *g*.

[43] Conduct (section 8).

The general result of these money transactions is, that Palmer appropriated to his own use all Cook's bets; that he tried to appropriate his stakes; and that shortly before, or just after his death, he was in possession of between £400 and £600, of which he paid Pratt £400, though very shortly before he was being pressed for money.

On Wednesday, November 21st, Mr. Jones went up to London, and informed Mr. Stephens, Cook's step-father, of his step-son's death. Mr. Stephens went to Lutterworth, found a will by which Cook appointed him his executor, and then went on to Rugeley, where he arrived about the middle of the day on Thursday.[44] He asked Palmer for information about Cook's affairs, and he replied, "There are £4,000 worth of bills out of his, and I am sorry to say my name is to them; but I have got a paper drawn up by a lawyer and signed by Mr. Cook to show that I never had any benefit from them." Mr. Stephens said that at all events he must be buried. Palmer offered to do so himself, and said that the body ought to be fastened up as soon as possible. The conversation then ended for the time. Palmer went out, and without authority from Mr. Stephens ordered a shell and a strong oak coffin.[45]

In the afternoon Mr. Stephens, Palmer, Jones, and a Mr. Bradford, Cook's brother-in-law, dined together, and after dinner Mr. Stephens desired Mr. Jones to fetch Cook's betting-book. Jones went to look for it, but was unable to find it. The betting-book had last been seen by the chambermaid. Mills, who gave it to Cook in bed on the Monday night, when he took a stamp from a pocket at the end of it. On hearing, that the book could not be found, Palmer said it was of no manner of use. Mr. Stephens said he understood Cook had won a great deal of money at Shrewsbury, to which Palmer replied, "It's no use, I assure you; when a man dies, his bets

[44] Introductory and explanatory (section 9).

[45] Admission and conduct (sections 17, 18; section 8).

are done with." He did not mention the fact that Cook's bets had been paid to Herring on the Monday. Mr. Stephens then said that the book must be found, and Palmer answered that no doubt it would be.[46] Before leaving the inn Mr. Stephens went to look at the body, before the coffin was fastened and observed that both hands were clenched. He returned at once to town and went to his attorney. He returned to Rugeley on Saturday, the 24th, and informed Palmer of his intention to have a post-mortem examination, which took place on Monday, 26th.[47]

The post-mortem examination was conducted in the presence of Palmer by Dr. Harland, Mr. Devonshire, a medical student, assisting Dr. Monkton, and Mr. Newton. The heart was contracted and empty. There were numerous small yellowish white spots, about the size of mustard-seed, at the larger end of the stomach. The upper part of the spinal cord was in its natural state; the lower part was not examined till the 25th January, when certain granules were found. There were many follicles on the tongue, apparently of long standing. The lungs appeared healthy to Dr. Harland, but Mr. Devonshire thought that there was some congestion.[48] Some points in Palmer's behaviour, both before and after the post-mortem examination, attracted notice. Newton said that on the Sunday night he sent for him, and asked what dose of strychnine would kill a dog. Newton said a grain. He asked whether it would be found in the stomach, and what would be the appearance of the stomach after death. Newton said there would be no inflammation, and he did not think it would be found. Newton thought he replied, "It's all right," as if speaking to himself, and added that he snapped his fingers. Whilst Devonshire was opening the

[46] These facts and statements together make it highly probable that Palmer stole the betting-book, which would be relevant as conduct (sections 8, 11).

[47] Introductory to what follows (section 9).

[48] Facts supporting opinions of experts (section 46).

stomach Palmer pushed against him, and part of the contents of the stomach was spilt. Nothing particular being found in the stomach, Palmer observed to Bamford, "They will not hang us yet." As they were all crowding together to see what passed, the push might have been an accident; and as Mr. Stephens' suspicions were well known, the remark was natural, though coarse. After the examination was completed, the intestines, &c., were put into a jar, over the top of which were tied two bladders. Palmer removed the jar from the table to a place near the door, and when it was missed said he thought it would be more convenient. When replaced it was found that a slit had been cut through both the bladders.[49]

After the examination Mr. Stephens and an attorney's clerk took the jars containing the viscera, &c., in a fly to Stafford.[50] Palmer asked the postboy if he was going to drive them to Stafford? The postboy said, "I believe I am." Palmer said, "Is it Mr. Stephens you are going to take?" He said, "I believe it is." Palmer said, "I suppose you are going to take the jars?" He said, "I am." Palmer asked if he would upset them? He said, "I shall not." Palmer said if he would there was a £10 note for him. He also said something about its being "a humbugging concern."[51] Some confusion was introduced into this evidence by the cross-examination, which tended to show that Palmer's object was to upset Mr. Stephens and not the jars, but at last the postboy (J. Myatt) repeated it as given above. Indeed, it makes little difference whether Palmer wished to upset Stephens or the jars, as they were all in one fly, and must be upset together if at all.

Shortly after the post-mortem examination an inquest was held before Mr. Ward, the coroner. It began on the 29th November and ended on the 5th December. On Sunday,

49 Conduct (section 8).

50 Introductory (section 9).

51 Conduct (section 8).

3rd December, Palmer asked Cheshire, the postmaster, "if he had anything fresh." Cheshire replied that he could not open a letter. Afterwards, however, he did open a letter from Dr. Alfred Taylor, who had analyzed the contents of the stomach, &c., to Mr. Gardiner, the attorney for the prosecution, and informed Palmer that Dr. Taylor said in that letter that no traces of strychnia were found. Palmer said he knew they would not, and he was quite innocent. Soon afterwards Palmer wrote to Mr. Ward, suggesting various questions to be put to witnesses at the inquest, and saying that he knew Dr. Taylor had told Mr. Gardiner there were no traces of strychnia, prussic acid, or opium. A few days before this, on the 1st December, Palmer had sent Mr. Ward, as a present, a codfish, a barrel of oysters, a brace of pheasants, and a turkey.[52] These circumstances certainly prove improper and even criminal conduct. Cheshire was imprisoned for his offence, and Lord Campbell spoke in severe terms of the conduct of the coroner; but a bad and unscrupulous man, as Palmer evidently was, might act in the manner described, even though he was innocent of the particular offence charged.

A medical book found in Palmer's possession had in it some MS. notes on the subject of strychnine, one of which was, "It kills by causing tetanic contraction of the respiratory muscles." It was not suggested that this memorandum was made for any particular purpose. It was used merely to show that Palmer was acquainted with the properties and effects of strychnine.[53]

This completes the evidence as to Palmer's behaviour before, at, and after the death of Cook. It proves beyond all question that, having the strongest possible motive to obtain at once a considerable sum of money, he robbed his friend of the whole of the bets paid to Herring on the Monday by a series of ingenious devices, and that he tried to rob him of the stakes; it raises the strongest presumption that he robbed

[52] Conduct and facts introductory thereto (sections 8, 9).

[53] Fact showing knowledge (section 14).

Cook of the £300 which, as Cook supposed, was sent up to Pratt on the 16th, and that he stole the money which he had on his person, and had received at Shrewsbury; it proves that he forged his name the night before he died, and that he tried to procure a fraudulent attestation to another forged document relating to his affairs the day after he died. It also proves that he had every opportunity of administering poison to Cook, that he told repeated lies about his state of health, and that he purchased deadly poison, for which he had no lawful use, on two separate occasions shortly before two paroxysms of a similar character to each other, the second of which deprived him of life.

The rest of the evidence was directed to prove that the symptoms of which Cook died were those of poisoning by strychnine, and that antimony, which was never prescribed for him, was found in his body. Evidence was also given in the course of the trial as to the state of Cook's health.

At the time of his death Cook was about twenty-eight years of age. Both his father and mother died young, and his sister and half-brother were not robust. He inherited from his father about £12,000 and was articled to a solicitor. Instead of following up that profession he betook himself to sporting pursuits, and appears to have led a rather dissipated life. He suffered from syphilis, and was in the habit of occasionally consulting Dr. Savage on the state of his health. Dr. Savage saw him in November, 1854, in May, in June, towards the end of October, and again early in November 1855, about a fortnight before his death, so that he had ample means of giving satisfactory evidence on the subject, especially as he examined him carefully whenever he came. Dr. Savage said that he had two shallow ulcers on the tongue corresponding to bad teeth; that he had also a sore throat, one of his tonsils being very large, red, and tender, and the other very small. Cook himself was afraid that these symptoms were syphilitic, but Dr. Savage thought decidedly that they were not. He also noticed "an indication of pulmonary affection under the left lung." Wishing to get him away from his turf associates, Dr. Savage recommended him to go abroad for the winter. His general health Dr. Savage considered good for a man who was not robust. Mr. Stephens said that when he last saw him alive he was looking better than he had looked for some time, and on his remarking, "You do not look anything of an invalid now," Cook struck himself on the breast, and said he was quite well. His friend, Mr. Jones also said that his health was generally good, though he was not very robust, and that he both hunted and played at cricket.[54]

On the other hand, witnesses were called for the prisoner who gave a different account of his health. A Mr. Sargent said he was with him at Liverpool a week before the Shrewsbury races, that he called his attention to the state of his mouth and throat, and the back part of his tongue was in a complete state of ulcer. "I said," added the witness, "I was surprised he could eat and drink in the state his mouth was in. He said he had been in that state for weeks and months, and now he did not take notice of it." This was certainly not consistent with Dr. Savage's evidence.[54]

Such being the state of health of Cook at the time of his death, the next question was as to its cause. The prosecution contended that the symptoms which attended it proved that he was poisoned by strichnia. Several eminent physicians and surgeons—Mr. Curling, Dr. Todd, Sir Benjamin Brodie, Mr. Daniel, and Mr. Solly—gave an account of the general character and causes of the disease of tetanus. Mr. Curling said that tetanus consists of spasmodic affection of the voluntary muscles of the body which at last ends in death, produced either by suffocation caused by the closing of the windpipe or by the wearing effect of the severe and painful struggles which the muscular spasms produce. Of this disease there are three forms,—idiopathic tetanus, which is produced with-

[54] State of things under which crime was committed (section 7).

out any assignable external cause; traumatic tetanus, which results from wounds; and the tetanus which is produced by the administration of strychnia, bruschia, and nux vomica, all of which are different forms of the same poison. Idiopathic tetanus is a very rare disease in England. Sir Benjamin Brodie had seen only one doubtful case of it. Mr. Daniel, who for twenty-eight years was surgeon to the Bristol Hospital, saw only two. Mr. Nunneley, professor of surgery at Leeds, had seen four. In India, however, it is comparatively common: Mr. Jackson, in twenty-five years' practice there, saw about forty cases. It was agreed on all hands, that though the exciting cause of the two diseases is different, their symptoms are the same. They were described in similar terms by several of the witnesses. Dr. Todd said the disease begins with stiffness about the jaw, the symptoms then extend themselves to the other muscles of the trunk and body. They gradually develop themselves. When once the disease has begun there are remissions of severity, but not complete intermission of the symptoms. In acute cases the disease terminates in three or four days. In chronic cases it will go on for as much as three weeks. There was some question as to what was the shortest case upon record. In a case mentioned by one of the prisoner's witnesses, Mr. Ross, the patient was said to have been attacked in the morning, either at eleven or some hours earlier, it did not clearly appear which, and to have died at half-past seven in the evening. This was the shortest case specified on either side, though its duration was not accurately determined. As a rule, however, tetanus, whether traumatic or idiopathic, was said to be a matter not of minutes, or even of hours, but of days.[55]

Such being the nature of tetanus, traumatic and idiopathic, four questions arose. Did Cook die of tetanus? Did he die of traumatic tetanus? Did he die of idiopathic tetanus? Did

[55] Opinions of experts, and facts on which they were founded (sections 45, 46). The rest of the evidence falls under this head.

he die of the tetanus produced by strychnia? The case for the prosecution upon these questions was, first, that he did die of tetanus. Mr. Curling said no doubt there was spasmodic action of the muscles (which was his definition of tetanus) in Cook's case; and even Mr. Nunnely, the principal witness for the prisoner, who contended that the death of Cook was caused neither by tetanus in its ordinary forms nor by the tetanus of strychnia, admitted that the paroxysm described by Mr. Jones was "very like" the paroxysm of tetanus. The close general resemblance of the symptoms to those of tetanus was indeed assumed by all the witnesses on both sides, as was proved by the various distinctions which were stated on the side of the Crown between Cook's symptoms and those of traumatic and idiopathic tetanus, and on the side of the prisoner between Cook's symptoms and the symptoms of the tetanus of strychnia. It might, therefore, be considered to be established that he died of tetanus in some form or other.

The next point asserted by the prosecution was, that he did not die of traumatic or idiopathic tetanus, because there was no wound on his body, and also because the course of the symptoms was different. They further asserted that the symptoms were those of poison by strychnia.

Upon these points the evidence was as follows:—Mr. Curling was asked, *Q.* "Were the symptoms consistent with "any form of traumatic tetanus which has ever come under "your knowledge or observation?" He answered, "No." *Q.* "What distinguished them from the cases of traumatic "tetanus which you have described?" *A.* "There was the "sudden onset of the fatal symptoms. In all cases that have "fallen under my notice the disease has been preceded by the "milder symptoms of tetanus." *Q.* "Gradually progressing to "their complete development, and completion, and death?" *A.* "Yes." He also mentioned "the sudden onset and rapid subsidence of the spasms" as inconsistent with the theory of either traumatic or idiopathic tetanus; and he said he had never known a case of tetanus which ran its course in less than eight or ten hours. In the one case which occupied so short a time, the true period could not be ascertained. In general, the time required was from one to several days. Sir Benjamin Brodie was asked, "In your opinion, are the symp- "toms those of traumatic tetanus or not?" He replied, "As "far as the spasmodic contraction of the muscles goes, the "symptoms resemble those of traumatic tetanus; as to the "course which the symptoms took, that was entirely dif- "ferent." He added, "The symptoms of traumatic tetanus "always begin, as far as I have seen, very gradually, the "stiffness of the lower jaw being, I believe, the symptom "first complained of—at least, so it has been in my experience; "then the contraction of the muscles of the back is always "a later symptom, generally much later; the muscles of the "extremities are affected in a much less degree than those of "the neck and trunk, except in some cases, where the injury "has been in a limb, and an early symptom has been a con- "traction of the muscles of that limb. I do not myself recol- "lect a case in which in ordinary tetanus there was that "contraction of the muscles of the hand which I under- "stand was stated to have existed in this instance. The "ordinary tetanus rarely runs its course in less that two or "three days, and often is protracted to a much longer "period; I know one case only in which the disease was said "to have terminated in twelve hours." He said, in conclu- sion, "I never saw a case in which the symptoms described "arose from any disease; when I say that, of course I refer "not to the particular symptoms, but to the general course "which the symptoms took." Mr. Daniel being asked whether the symptoms of Cook could be referred to idiopathic or trau- matic tetanus, said, "In my judgment they could not." He also said that he should repeat Sir Benjamin Brodie's words if he were to enumerate the distinctions. Mr. Solly said that the symptoms were not referable to any disease he ever witnessed; and Dr. Todd said, "I think the symptoms were those of strychnia." The same opinion was expressed with equal confidence by Dr. Alfred Taylor, Dr. Rees, and Mr. Christison.[54]

In order to support this general evidence witnesses were called who gave account of three fatal cases of poisoning by strychnia, and of one case in which the patient recovered. The first of the fatal cases was that of Agnes French, or Senet, who was accidentally poisoned at Glasgow Infirmary, in 1845, by some pills which she took, and which were intended for a paralytic patient. According to the nurse, the girl was taken ill three quarters of an hour, according to one of the physicians (who, however, was not present) twenty minutes after she swallowed the pills. She fell suddenly back on the floor; when her clothes were cut off she was stiff, "just like a poker," her arms were stretched out, her hands clenched; she vomited slightly; she had no lockjaw; there was a retraction of the mouth and face, the head was bent back, the spine curved. She went into severe paroxysms every few seconds, and died about an hour after the symptoms began. She was perfectly conscious. The heart was found empty on examination.

The second case described was that of Mrs. Serjeantson Smyth, who was accidentally poisoned at Romsey in 1848, by strychnine put into a dose of ordinary medicine instead of salicine. She took the dose about five or ten minutes after seven; in five or ten minutes more the servant was alarmed by a violent ringing of the bell. She found her mistress leaning on a chair, went out to send for a doctor, and on her return found her on the floor. She screamed loudly. She asked to have her legs pulled straight and to have water thrown over her. A few minutes before she died she said, "Turn me over;" she was turned over, and died very quietly almost immediately. The fit lasted about an hour. The hands were clenched, the feet contracted, and on a post-mortem examination the heart was found empty.

The third case was that of Mrs. Dove, who was poisoned

at Leeds by her husband (for which he was afterwards hanged) in February, 1856. She had five attacks on the Monday Wednesday, Thursday, Friday, and Saturday of the week beginning February 24th. She had prickings in the legs and twitchings in the hands. She asked her husband to rub her arms and legs before the spasms came on, but when they were strong she could not bear her legs to be touched. The fatal attack in her case lasted two hours and a half. The hands were semi-bent, the feet strongly arched. The lungs were congested, the spinal cord was also much congested. The head being opened first, a good deal of blood flowed out, part of which might flow from the heart.

The case in which the patient recovered was that of a paralytic patient of Mr. Moore's. He took an over dose of strychnia, and in about three quarters of an hour Mr. Moore found him stiffened in every limb. His head was drawn back; he was screaming and "frequently requesting that we should turn him, move him, rub him." His spine was drawn back. He snapped at a spoon with which an attempt was made to administer medicine, and was perfectly conscious during the whole time.

Dr. Taylor and Dr. Owen Rees examined Cook's body. They found no strychnia, but they found antimony in the liver, the left kidney, the spleen, and also in the blood.

The case for the prosecution upon this evidence was, that the symptoms were those of tetanus, and of tetanus produced by strychnia. The case for the prisoner was, first, that several of the symptoms observed were inconsistent with strychnia; and secondly, that all of them might be explained on other hypotheses. Their evidence was given in part by their own witnesses, and in part by the witnesses for the Crown in cross-examination. The replies suggested by the Crown were founded partly on the evidence of their own witnesses given by way of anticipation, and partly by the evidence obtained from the witnesses for the prisoner on cross-examination.

The first and most conspicuous argument on behalf of the prisoner was, that the fact that no strychnia was discovered by Dr. Taylor and Dr. Rees was inconsistent with the theory that any had been administered. The material part of Dr. Taylor's evidence upon this point was, that he had examined the stomach and intestines of Cook for a variety of poisons, strychnia among others, without success. The contents of the stomach were gone, though the contents of the intestines remained, and the stomach itself had been cut open from end to end, and turned inside out, and the mucous surface on which poison, if present, would have been found was rubbing against the surface of the intestines. This Dr. Taylor considered a most unfavourable condition for the discovery of poison, and Mr. Christison agreed with him. Several of the prisoner's witnesses, on the contrary—Mr. Nunneley, Dr. Letheby, and Mr. Rogers,—thought that it would only increase the difficulty of the operation, and not destroy its chance of success.

Apart from this Dr. Taylor expressed his opinion that from the way in which strychnia acts, it might be impossible to discover it even if the circumstances were favourable. The mode of testing its presence in the stomach is to treat the stomach in various ways, until at last a residue is obtained which, upon the application of certain chemical ingredients, changes its colour if strychnia is present. All the witnesses agreed that strychnia acts by absorption—that is, it is taken up from the stomach by the absorbents, thence it passes into the blood, thence into the solid part of the body, and at some stage of its progress causes death by its action on the nerves and muscles. Its noxious effects do not begin till it has left the stomach. From this Dr. Taylor argued that if a minimum dose were administered, none would be left in the stomach at the time of death, and therefore none could be discovered there. He also said that if the strychnia got into the blood before examination, it would be diffused over the whole mass, and so no more than an extremely minute portion would be present in any given quantity. If the dose were half a grain, and there were twenty-five pounds of blood in the body, each pound of blood would contain only one-fiftieth of a grain. He was also of opinion that the strychnia undergoes some chemical change by reason of which its presence in small quantities in the tissues cannot be detected. In short, the result of his evidence was, that if a minimum dose were administered, it was uncertain whether strychnia would be present in the stomach after death, and that if it was not in the stomach, there was no certainty that it could be found at all. He added that he considered the colour tests fallacious, because the colours might be produced by other substances.

Dr. Taylor further detailed some experiments which he had tried upon animals jointly with Dr. Rees, for the purpose of ascertaining whether strychnia could always be detected. He poisoned four rabbits with strychnia, and applied the tests for strychnia to their bodies. In one case, where two grains had been administered at intervals, he obtained proof of the presence of strychnia both by a bitter taste and by the colour. In a case where one grain was administered, he obtained the taste but not the colour. In the other two cases, where he administered one grain and half a grain respectively, he obtained no indications at all of the presence of strychnia. These experiments proved to demonstration that the fact that *he* did not discover strychnia did not prove that no strychnia was present in Cook's body.

Mr. Nunneley, Mr. Herapath, Mr. Rogers, Dr. Letheby and Mr. Wrightson contradicted Dr. Taylor and Dr. Rees upon this part of their evidence. They denied the theory that strychnine undergoes any change in the blood, and they professed their own ability to discover its presence even in most minute quantities in any body into which it had been introduced, and their belief that the colour tests were satisfactory. Mr. Herapath said that he had found strychnine in the blood and in a small part of the liver of a dog poisoned by it; and he also said that he could detect the fifty-thousandth part of a grain if it were unmixed with organic matter. Mr. Wrightson (who was highly complimented by Lord Campbell for the way in which he gave his evidence) also said that he should expect to find strychnia if it were present, and that he had found it in the tissues of an animal poisoned by it.

Here, no doubt, there was a considerable conflict of evidence upon a point on which it was very difficult for unscientific persons to pretend to have any opinion. The evidence given for the prisoner however tended to prove not so much that there was no strychnia in Cook's body, as that Dr. Taylor ought to have found it if there was. In other words, it had less to do with the guilt or innocence of the prisoner, than with the question whether Mr. Nunneley and Mr. Herapath were or were not better analytical chemists than Dr. Taylor. The evidence could not even be considered to shake Dr. Taylor's credit, for no part of the case rested on his evidence except the discovery of the antimony, as to which he was corroborated by Mr. Brande, and was not contradicted by the prisoner's witnesses. His opinion as to the nature of Cook's symptoms was shared by many other medical witnesses of the highest eminence, whose credit was altogether unimpeached. The prisoner's counsel were placed in a curious difficulty by this state of the question. They had to attack and did attack Dr. Taylor's credit vigorously for the purpose of rebutting his conclusion that Cook might have been poisoned by strychnine; yet they had also to maintain his credit as a skilful analytical chemist, for if they destroyed it, the fact that he did not find strychnine went for nothing. This dilemma was fatal. To admit his skill was to admit their client's guilt. To deny it was to destroy the value of nearly all their own evidence. The only possible course was to admit his skill and deny his good faith, but this too was useless for the reason just mentioned.

Another argument used on behalf of the prisoner was that some of the symptoms of Cook's death were inconsistent with poisoning by strychnine. Mr. Nunneley and Dr. Letheby thought that the facts that Cook sat up in bed when the attack came on, that he moved his hands, and swallowed, and asked to be rubbed and moved, showed more power of voluntary motion than was consistent with poisoning by strychnia. But Mrs. Serjeantson Smyth got out of bed and rang the bell, and both she, Mrs. Dove, and Mr. Moore's patient begged to be rubbed and moved before the spasms came on. Cook's movements were before the paroxysm set in, and the first paroxysm ended his life.

Mr. Nunneley referred to the fact that the heart was empty, and said that, in his experiments, he always found that the right side of the heart of the poisoned animals was full.

Both in Mrs. Smyth's case, however, and in that of the girl Senet, the heart was found empty; and in Mrs. Smyth's case the chest and abdomen were opened first, so that the heart was not emptied by the opening of the head. Mr. Christison said that if a man died of spasms of the heart, the heart would be emptied by them, and would be found empty after death, so that the presence or absence of the blood proved nothing.

Mr. Nunneley and Dr. Letheby also referred to the length of time before the symptoms appeared, as inconsistent with poisoning by strychnine. The time between the administration of the pills and the paroxysm was not accurately measured. It might have been an hour, or a little less, or more; but the poison, if present at all, was administered in pills, which would not begin to operate till they were broken up, and the rapidity with which they would be broken up would depend upon the materials of which they were made Mr. Christison said that if the pills were made up with resinous materials, such as are within the knowledge of every medical man, their operation would be delayed. He added, "I do not think we can fix, with our present knowledge, the "precise time for the poison beginning to operate." According to the account of one witness in Agnes French's case, the poison did not operate for three quarters of an hour, though probably her recollection of the time was not very accurate after ten years. Dr. Taylor also referred (in cross-examination) to cases in which an hour and a half, or even two hours elapsed, before the symptoms showed themselves.

These were the principal points in Cook's symptoms said to be inconsistent with the administration of strychnia. All of them appear to have been satisfactorily answered. Indeed, the inconsistency of the symptoms with strychnia was faintly maintained. The defence turned rather on the possibility of showing that they were consistent with some other disease.

In order to make out this point various suggestions were made. In the cross-examination of the different witnesses for the Crown, it was frequently suggested that the case was one of traumatic tetanus, caused by syphilitic sores; but to this there were three fatal objections. In the first place, there were no syphilitic sores; in the second place, no witness for the prisoner said that he thought that it was a case of traumatic tetanus; and in the third place, several doctors of great experience in respect of syphilis—especially Dr. Lee, the physician to the Lock Hospital—declared that they never heard of syphilitic sores producing tetanus. Two witnesses for the prisoner were called to show that a man died of tetanus who had sores on his elbow and elsewhere, which were possibly syphilitic; but it did not appear whether he had rubbed or hurt them, and Cook had no symptoms of the sort.

Another theory was that the death was caused by general convulsions. This was advanced by Mr. Nunneley; but he was unable to mention any case in which general convulsions had produced death without destroying consciousness. He said vaguely he had heard of such cases, but had never met with one. Dr. McDonald, of Garnkirk, near Glasgow, said that he considered the case to be one of "epileptic convulsions with tetanic complications." But he also failed to mention an instance in which epilepsy did not destroy consciousness. This witness assigned the most extraordinary reasons for supposing that it was a case of this form of epilepsy. He said that the fit might have been caused by sexual excitement, though the man was ill at Rugeley for nearly a week before his death; and that it was within the range of possibility that sexual intercourse might produce a convulsion fit after an interval of a fortnight.

Both Mr. Nunneley and Dr. McDonald were cross-examined with great closeness. Each of them was taken separately through all the various symptoms of the case, and asked to point out how they differed from those of poisoning by strychnia, and what were the reasons why they should be supposed to arise from anything else. After a great deal of trouble, Mr. Nunneley was forced to admit that the symptoms of the paroxysm were "very like" those of strychnia, and that the various predisposing causes which he mentioned as likely to produce convulsions could not be shown to have existed. He said, for instance, that excitement and depression of spirits might predispose to convulsions; but the only excitement under which Cook had laboured was on winning the race a week before; and as for depression of spirits, he was laughing and joking with Mr. Jones a few hours before his death. Dr. McDonald was equally unable to give a satisfactory explanation of these difficulties. It is impossible by any abridgment to convey the full effect which these cross-examinations produced. They deserve to be carefully studied by any one who cares to understand the full effect of this great instrument for the manifestation not merely of truth, but of accuracy and fairness.

Of the other witnesses for the prisoner, Mr. Herapath admitted that he had said that he thought that there was strychnine in the body, but that Dr. Taylor did not know how to find it. He added that he got his impression from newspaper reports; but it did not appear that they differed from the evidence given at the trial. Dr. Letheby said that the symptoms of Cook were irreconcilable with everything that he was acquainted with—strychnia poison included. He admitted, however, that they were not inconsistent with what he had heard of the symptoms of Mrs. Serjeantson Smyth who was undoubtedly poisoned by strychnine. Mr. Partridge was called to show that the case might be one of arachnitis, or inflammation of one of the membranes of the spinal cord caused by two granules discovered there. In cross-examination he instantly admitted, with perfect frankness, that he did not think the case was one of arachnitis, as the symptoms were not the same. Moreover, on being asked whether the symptoms described by Mr. Jones were consistent with poisoning by strychnia, he said, "Quite;" and he concluded by saying that in the whole course of his experience and knowledge he had never seen such a death proceed from natural causes. Dr. Robinson, from Newcastle, was called to show that tetanic convulsions preceded by epilepsy were the cause of death. He, however, expressly admitted in cross-examination that the symptoms were consistent with strychnia, and that some of them were inconsistent with epilepsy. He said that in the absence of any other cause, if he "put aside the hypothesis of strychnia," he would ascribe it to epilepsy; and that he thought the granules in the spinal cord might have produced epilepsy. The degree of importance attached to these granules by different witnesses varied. Several of the witnesses for the Crown considered them unimportant. The last of the prisoner's witnesses was Dr. Richardson, who said the disease might have been angina pectoris. He said, however, that the symptoms of angina pectoris were so like those of strychnine that he should have great difficulty in distinguishing them from each other.

The fact that antimony was found was never seriously disputed, nor could it be denied that its administration would account for all the symptoms of sickness, &c., which occurred during the week before Cook's death. No one but the prisoner could have administered it.

The general result of the whole evidence on both sides appears to be to prove beyond all reasonable doubt that the symptoms of Cook's death were perfectly consistent with those of poisoning by strychnine, and that there was strong reason to believe that they were inconsistent with any other cause. Coupling this with the proof that Palmer bought strychnia just before each of the two attacks, and that he robbed Cook of all his property, it is impossible to doubt the propriety of the verdict.

Remarks on Palmer's case.

Palmer's case is remarkable on account of the extraordinary minuteness and labour with which it was tried, and on account of the extreme ability with which the trial was conducted on both sides.

The intricate set of facts which show that Palmer had a strong motive to commit the crime; his behaviour before it, at the time when it was being committed, and after it had been committed; the various considerations which showed that Cook must have died by tetanus produced by strychnine; that Palmer had the means of administering strychnine to him; that he did actually administer what in all probability was strychnine; that he also administered antimony on many occasions; and that all the different theories by which Cook's death otherwise than by strychnine could be accounted for were open to fatal objections, form a collection of eight or ten different sets of facts, all connected together immediately or remotely either as being, or as being shown not to be, the causes or the effects of Cook's murder, or as forming part of the actual murder itself.

The scientific evidence is remarkable on various grounds, but particularly because it supplies a singularly perfect illustration of the identity between the ordinary processes of scientific research, and the principles explained above as being those on which Judicial Evidence proceeds. Take for instance the question, Did Cook die of tetanus, either traumatic or idiopathic? The symptoms of those diseases are in the first place ascertained inductively, and their nature was proved by the testimony of Sir Benjamin Brodie and others. The course of the symptoms being compared with those of Cook, they did not correspond. The inference by deduction was that Cook's death was not caused by those diseases. Logically the matter might be stated thus:—

All persons who die either of traumatic or of idiopathic tetanus exhibit a certain course of symptoms.

Cook did not exhibit that course of symptoms, therefore Cook did not die of traumatic or of idiopathic tetanus.

Every one of the arguments and theories stated in the case may easily be shown by a little attention to be so many illustrations of the rules of evidence on the one hand, and of the rules of induction and deduction on the other.

On the other hand, a flood of irrelevant matter apparently connected with the trial pressed, so to speak, for admittance, and if it had been admitted, would have swollen the trial to unmanageable proportions, and thrown no real light upon the main question. Palmer was actually indicted for the murder of his wife, Ann Palmer, and for the murder of his brother, Walter Palmer. Every sort of story was in circulation as to what he had done. It was said that twelve or fourteen persons had at different times been buried from his house under suspicious circumstances. It was said that he had poisoned Lord George Bentinck, who died very suddenly some years before. He had certainly forged his mother's acceptance to bills of exchange, and had carried on a series of gross frauds on insurance offices. There was the strongest reason to suspect that the evidence of Jeremiah Smith, referred to in the case was plotted and artful perjury. If Palmer had been tried in France, every one of these and innumerable other topics would have been introduced, and the real matter in dispute would not have been nearly so fully discussed.

No case sets in a clearer light either the theory or the practical working of the principles on which the Evidence Act is based.

One special matter on which Palmer's trial throws great light is the nature of the evidence of experts. The provisions relating to this subject are contained in Sections 45 and 46 of the Evidence Act. The only point of much importance in connection with them is that it should be borne in mind that their evidence is given on the assumption that certain facts occurred, but that it does not in common cases show whether or not the facts on which the expert gives his opinion did really occur. For instance, Sir Benjamin Brodie and other witnesses in Palmer's case said that the symptoms they had heard described were the symptoms of poisoning by strychnine, but whether the maid-servants and others who witnessed and des cribed Cook's death were or were not speaking the truth was not a question for them, but for the jury. Strictly speaking, an expert ought not to be asked, "Do you think that the deceased man died of poison?" He ought to be asked to what cause he would attribute the death of the deceased man, assuming the symptoms attending his death to have been correctly described? or whether any cause except poison would account for such and such specified symptoms? This, however, is a matter of form. The substance of the rules as to experts is that they are only witnesses, not judges; that their evidence, however important, is intended to be used only as materials upon which others are to form their decision; and that the fact which they have to prove is the fact that they entertain certain opinions on certain grounds, and not the fact that grounds for their opinions do really exist.

Irrelevant Facts.

Having thus described and illustrated the theory of relevancy, it will be desirable to say something of irrelevant facts which might at first sight be supposed to be relevant.

From the explanations given in the earlier part of the chapter it follows that facts are irrelevant unless they can be shown to stand in the relation of cause or in the relation of effect to facts in issue, every step in the connection being either proved or of such a nature that it may be presumed without proof.

What facts are irrelevant.

The vast majority of ordinary facts simply coexist without being in any assignable manner connected together. For instance, at the moment of the commission of a crime in a great city numberless other transactions are going on in the immediate neighbourhood; but no one would think of giving evidence of them unless they were in some way connected with the crime. Facts obviously irrelevant therefore present little difficulty. The only difficulty arises in dealing with facts which are apparently relevant but are not really so. The most important of these are three :—

Facts apparently relevant.

1. Statements as to facts made by persons not called as witnesses.

2. Transactions similar to but unconnected with the facts in issue.

3. Opinions formed by persons as to the facts in issue or relevant facts.

None of these are relevant within the definition of relevancy given in Sections 6—11, both inclusive. It may possibly be argued that the effect of the second paragraph of Section 11 *

* Section 11 is as follows :—

Facts not otherwise relevant are relevant.

(1) If they are inconsistent with any fact in issue or relevant fact.

would be to admit proof of such facts as these. It may, for instance, be said: A (not called as a witness) was heard to declare that he had seen B commit a crime. This makes it highly probable that B did commit that crime. Therefore A's declaration is a relevant fact under Section 11 (2). This was not the intention of the section, as is shown by the elaborate provisions contained in the following part of the Chapter II. (Sections 12—39) as to particular classes of statements, which are regarded as relevant facts either because the circumstances under which they are made invest them with importance, or because no better evidence can be got. The sort of facts which the section was intended to include are facts which either exclude or imply more or less distinctly the existence of the facts sought to be proved. Some degree of latitude was designedly left in the wording of the section (in compliance with a suggestion from the Madras Government) on account of the variety of matters to which it might apply. The meaning of the section would have been more fully expressed if words to the following effect had been added to it:—

"No statement shall be regarded as rendering the matter stated highly probable within the meaning of this section unless it is declared to be a relevant fact under some other section of this Act."

Reason for exclusion of hearsay.

The reasons why statements as to facts made by persons not called as witnesses are excluded, except in certain specified cases (see Sections 17—39), are various. In the first place it is matter of common experience that statements in common conversation are made so lightly, and are so liable to be misunderstood or misrepresented, that they cannot be depended upon for any important purpose unless they are made under special circumstances.

---

(2) If by themselves, or in connection with other facts, they make the existence or non-existence of any fact in issue or relevant fact highly probable or improbable.

Objection.

It may be said that this is an objection to the weight of such statements and not to their relevancy, and there is some degree of truth in this remark. No doubt, when a man has to inquire into facts of which he receives in the first instance very confused accounts, it may and often will be extremely important for him to trace the most cursory and apparently futile report. And facts relevant in the highest degree to facts in issue may often be discovered in this manner. A policeman or a lawyer engaged in getting up a case, criminal or civil, would neglect his duty altogether if he shut his ears to everything which was not relevant within the meaning of the Evidence Act. A judge or magistrate in India frequently has to perform duties which in England would be performed by police officers or attorneys. He has to sift out the truth for himself as well as he can, and with little assistance of a professional kind. Section 165 is intended to arm the judge with the most extensive power possible for the purpose of getting at the truth. The effect of this section,* is that in order to get to the bottom of the matter before it the court will be able to look at and inquire into every fact whatever. It will not, however, be able to found its judgment upon the class of statements in question, for the following reasons.

Effect of section 165.

If this were permitted it would present a great temptation to indolent judges to be satisfied with second-hand reports.

It would open a wide door to fraud. People would make statements for which they would be in no way responsible, and the fact that these statements were made would be proved by witnesses who knew nothing of the matter stated. Every one would thus be at the mercy of people who might choose to tell a lie, and whose evidence could neither be tested nor contradicted.

* Section 165 is as follows:

"The judge may in order to discover or obtain proper proof of "relevant facts ask any question he pleases in any form, at any time, "of any witness, or of the parties about any fact relevant or irrele- "vant, and may order the production of any document or thing."

Suppose that A, B, C, and D give to E, F, and G a minute detailed account of a crime which they say was committed by Z. E, F, and G repeat what they have heard correctly. A, B, C, and D disappear or are not forthcoming. It is evident that Z would be altogether unable to defend himself in this case, and that the court would be unable to test the statements of A, B, C, and D. The only way to avoid this is to exclude such evidence altogether, and so to put upon both judges and magistrates as strong a pressure as possible to get to the bottom of the matter before them.

It would waste an incalculable amount of time. To try to trace unauthorized and irresponsible gossip, and to discover the grains of truth which may lurk in it is like trying to trace a fish in the water.

Unconnected transactions.

The exclusion of evidence as to transactions similar to, but not specifically connected with the facts in issue, rests upon the ground that if it were not enforced every trial, whether civil or criminal, might run into an inquiry into the whole life and character of the parties concerned. Litigants have frequently many matters in difference besides the precise point legally at issue between them, and it often requires a good deal of vigour to prevent them from turning courts of justice into theatres in which all their affairs may be discussed. A very slight acquaintance with French procedure is enough to show the evils of not keeping people close to the point in judicial proceedings.

Exclusion of Evidence of opinion.

As to evidence of opinion, it is excluded because its admission would in nearly all cases be mere waste of time.

Exceptions to rules as to irrelevancy

The concluding part of the chapter on the relevancy of facts enumerates the exceptions which are to be made to the general rules as to irrelevancy. The rules as to admissions, statements made by persons who cannot be called as witnesses, and statements made under circumstances which in themselves afford a guarantee for their truth, are an exception to the exclusion of statements as proof of the matter stated.

Judgments in courts of justice on other occasions form an

exception to the exclusion of evidence of transactions not specifically connected with facts in issue, and the provisions as to the admission of evidence of opinions in certain cases are contained in Sections 45—55. I will notice very shortly the principle on which these provisions proceed.

Admissions.

1. The general rule with regard to admissions, which are defined to mean all that the parties or their representatives in certain degrees say about the matter in dispute, or facts relevant thereto, is that they may be proved as against those who made them, but not in their favour. The reason of the rule is obvious. If A says, "B owes me money," the mere fact that he says so does not even tend to prove the debt. If the statement has any value at all, it must be derived from some fact which lies beyond it; for instance, A's recollection of his having lent B the money. To that fact, of course, A can testify, but his subsequent assertions add nothing to what he has to say. If, on the other hand, A had said, "B does not owe me anything," this is a fact of which B might make use, and which might be decisive of the case.

Confessions.

Admissions in reference to crimes are usually called confessions. I may observe upon the provisions relating to them that Sections 25, 26, and 27 were transferred to the Evidence *verbatim* from the Code of Criminal Procedure, Act xxv. of 1861. They differ widely from the law of England, and were inserted in the Act of 1861 in order to prevent the practice of torture by the police for the purpose of extracting confessions from persons in their custody.

Statements by witnesses who cannot be called.

Statements made by persons who are dead or otherwise incapacitated from being called as witnesses are admitted in the cases mentioned in Sections 32 and 33. The reason is that in the cases in question no better evidence is to be had.

Statements under special circumstances.

In certain cases statements are made under circumstances which in themselves are a strong reason for believing them to be true, and in these cases there is generally little use in calling the person by whom the statement was made. The sections which relate to them are 34—38.

It may be well to point out here the manner in which the Evidence Act affects the proof of evidence given by a witness in a court of justice. The relevancy of the fact that such evidence was given, depends partly on the general principles of relevancy. For instance, if a witness were accused of giving false testimony, the fact that he gave the testimony alleged to be false would be a fact in issue. But the Act also provides for cases in which the fact that evidence was given on a different occasion is to be admissible, either to prove the matter stated (Section 33), or in order to contradict (Sections 155, 3) or in order to corroborate (Section 157) the witness. By reference to these Sections it must be ascertained whether the fact that the evidence was given is relevant. If it is relevant, Section 35 enacts that an entry of it in a record made by any public servant in the discharge of his duty shall be relevant as a mode of proving it. The Codes of Civil and Criminal Procedure direct all judicial officers to make records of the evidence given before them; and Section 80 of the Evidence Act provides that a document purporting to be a record of evidence shall be presumed to be genuine, that statements made as to the circumstances under which it was taken shall be presumed to be true, and the evidence to have been duly taken. The result of these sections taken together is that when proof of evidence given on previous occasions is admissible, it may be proved by the production of the record or a certified copy (see Section 76).

Judgments in other cases.

The sections as to judgments (40, 41) designedly omit to deal with the question of the effect of judgments in preventing further proceedings in regard of the same matter. The law upon this subject is to be found in Section 2 of the Code of Civil Procedure, and in Section of 460 the Code of Criminal Procedure. The cases which the Evidence Act provides for are cases in which the judgment of a court is in the nature of a law, and creates the right which it affirms to exist.

Opinions.

The opinions of any persons, other than the judge by whom the fact is to be decided, as to the existence of facts in issue or relevant facts are, as a rule, irrelevant to the decision of the cases to which they relate, for the most obvious reasons. To show that such and such a person thought that a crime had been committed or a contract made would either be to show nothing at all, or it would invest the person whose opinion was proved with the character of a judge. In some few cases, the reasons for which are self-evident, it is otherwise. They are specified in Sections 45—51.

Character when important.

The sections as to character require little remark. Evidence of character is, generally speaking, only a makeweight, though there are two classes of cases in which it is highly important :—

(1) Where conduct is equivocal, or even presumably criminal In this case evidence of character may explain conduct and rebut the presumptions which it might raise in the absence of such evidence. A man is found in possession of stolen goods. He says he found them and took charge of them to give them to the owner. If he is a man of very high character this may be believed.

(2) When a charge rests on the direct testimony of a single witness, and on the bare denial of it by the person charged. A man is accused of an indecent assault by a woman with whom he was accidentally left alone. He denies it. Here a high character for morality on the part of the accused person would be of great importance.

CHAPTER IV.

GENERAL OBSERVATIONS ON THE INDIAN EVIDENCE ACT.

CHAP. V. No reference to English cases.

IN the preceding pages I have stated and illustrated the theory of judicial evidence on which the Evidence Act is based. I have but little to add to that explanation. The Act speaks for itself. No labour was spared to make its provisions complete and distinct. As the first section repeals all unwritten rules of evidence, and as the Act itself supplies a distinct body of law upon the subject, its object would be defeated by elaborate references to English cases. In so far as it is obscure or incomplete, the judges and the Legislature are its proper critics. If it is turned into an abridgment of the law which it was meant to replace, it will be injurious instead of being useful to those for whom it was intended.

I shall accordingly content myself with a very short description of the contents of the remainder of the Act, referring for a full explanation of the matter to the Act itself.

Scheme of Part II.

The general scheme of Part II., which relates to Proof and consists of four chapters, containing forty-five sections, may be expressed in the following propositions:—

Judicial notice.

1. Certain facts are so notorious in themselves, or are stated in so authentic a manner in well-known and accessible publications, that they require no proof. The court, if it does not know them, can inform itself upon them without formally taking evidence. These facts are said to be judicially noticed.

Oral evidence.

2. All facts except the contents of documents may be proved by oral evidence, which must in all cases be direct. That is, it must consist of a declaration by the witness that he perceived by his own senses the fact to which he testifies.

CHAP. IV. Documents.

3. The contents of documents must be proved either by the production of the document, which is called primary evidence, or by copies or oral accounts of the contents, which are called secondary evidence. Primary evidence is required as a rule, but this is subject to seven important exceptions in which secondary evidence may be given. The most important of these are (1) cases in which the document is in the possession of the adverse party, in which case the adverse party must in general (though there are several exceptions) have notice to produce the document before secondary evidence of it can be given.

And (2) cases in which certified copies of public documents are admissible in place of the documents themselves.

4. Many classes of documents which are defined in the act, are presumed to be what they purport to be, but this presumption is liable to be rebutted. Two sets of presumptions will sometimes apply to the same document. For instance what purports to be a certified copy of a record of evidence is produced. It must by Section 76 be presumed to be an accurate copy of the record of evidence. By Section 80 the facts stated in the record itself as to the circumstances under which it was taken, *e.g.*, that it was read over to the witness in a language which he understood, must be presumed to be true.

Writings when exclusive evidence.

5. When a contract, grant, or other disposition of property is reduced to writing, the writing itself (or secondary evidence of its contents) is not only the best but is the only admissible evidence of the matter which it contains. It cannot be varied by oral evidence, except in certain specified cases.

It is necessary in applying these general doctrines (the expediency of which is obvious) to practice to go into considerable detail, and to introduce provisos, exceptions, and qualifications which appear more intricate and difficult than they really are. If, however, the propositions just stated are once distinctly understood and borne in mind, the details will be easily mastered when the occasion for applying them arises. The provisions in the Act are all made in order to meet real difficulties which arose in practice in England, and which must of necessity arise over and over again, and give occasion to litigation unless they were specifically provided for beforehand.

Principle of provisions in documentary evidence.

One single principle runs through all the propositions relating to documentary evidence. It is that the very object for which writing is used is to perpetuate the memory of what is written down, and so to furnish permanent proof of it. In order that full effect may be given to this, two things are necessary, namely, that the document itself should whenever it is possible be put before the judge for his inspection, and that if it purports to be a final settlement of a previous negotiation, as in the case of a written contract, it shall be treated as final, and shall not be varied by word of mouth. If the first of these rules were not observed the benefit of writing would be lost. There is no use in writing a thing down unless the writing is read. If the second rule were not observed people would never know when a question was settled, as they would be able to play fast and loose with their writings.

By bearing these leading principles in mind the details and exceptions will become simple. Their practical importance is indeed as nothing in comparison to the importance of the rules which they qualify.

The third part of the Act, which contains three chapters (Chapters VII., VIII., and IX.) and sixty-seven sections, relates to the production and effect of evidence.

Presumptions.

Chapter VII., which relates to the burden of proof, deals with a subject which requires a little explanation. This is the subject of presumptions. Like most other words introduced into the law of evidence, it has various meanings, and it has besides a history to which I shall refer very shortly.

In times when the true theory of proof was very imperfectly understood, inasmuch as physical science, by the progress of which that theory was gradually discovered, was in its infancy, numerous attempts were made to construct theories

CHAP. IV. as to the weight of evidence which should supply the want of one founded on observation. In some cases this was effected by requiring the testimony of a certain number of witnesses in particular cases; such a fact must be proved by two witnesses, such another by four, and so on. In other cases particular items of evidence were regarded as full proof, half full proof, proof less than half full, and proof more than half full.

The doctrine of presumptions was closely connected with this theory. Presumptions were inferences which the judges were directed to draw from certain states of facts in certain cases, and these presumptions were allowed a certain amount of weight in the scale of proof; such a presumption and such evidence amounted to full proof, such another to half full, and so on. The very irregular manner in which the English law of evidence grew up has had, amongst other effects, that of making it an uncertain and difficult question how far the theory of presumptions, and the other theories of which they formed a part, affect English law, but substantially the result is somewhat as follows:—

Presumptions are of four kinds according to English law.

1. Conclusive presumptions. These are rare, but when they occur they provide that certain modes of proof shall not be liable to contradiction.

2. Presumptions which affect the ordinary rule as to the burden of proof that he who affirms must prove. He who affirms that a man is dead must usually prove it, but if he shows that the man has not been heard of for seven years, he shifts the burden of proof on his adversary.

3. There are certain presumptions which, though liable to be rebutted, are regarded by English law as being something more than mere maxims, though it is by no means easy to say how much more. An instance of such a presumption is to be found in the rule that recent possession of stolen goods unexplained raises a presumption that the possessor is either the thief or a receiver.

4. Bare presumptions of fact, which are nothing but arguments to which the Court attaches whatever value it pleases. CHAP. IV.

Chapter VII. of the Evidence Act deals with this subject as follows:—First it lays down the general principles which regulate the burden of proof (sections 101—106). It then enumerates the cases in which the burden of proof is determined in particular cases, not by the relation of the parties to the cause, but by presumptions (sections 107—111). It notices two cases of conclusive presumptions, the presumption of legitimacy from birth during marriage (section 112), and the presumption of a valid cession of territory from the publication of a notification to that effect in the *Gazette of India* (section 113). This is one of several conclusive statutory presumptions which will be found in different parts of the statutes and Acts. Finally, it declares, in section 114, that the court may in all cases whatever draw from the facts before it whatever inferences it thinks just. The terms of this section are such as to reduce to their proper position of mere maxims which are to be applied to facts by the courts in their discretion, a large number of presumptions to which English law gives, to a greater or less extent, an artificial value. Nine of the most important of them are given by way of illustration.

All notice of certain general legal principles which are, sometimes called presumptions, but which in reality belong rather to the substantive law than to the law of evidence, was designedly omitted, not because the truth of those principles was denied, but because it was not considered that the Evidence Act was the proper place for them. The most important of these is the presumption, as it is sometimes called, that every one knows the law. The principle is far more correctly stated in the maxim, that ignorance of the law does not excuse a breach of it, which is one of the fundamental principles of criminal law.

The subject of estoppels (Chapter VIII,.) differs from that

CHAP. IV. of presumptions in the circumstance that an estoppel is a personal disqualification laid upon a person peculiarly circumstanced from proving peculiar facts. A presumption is a rule that particular inferences shall be drawn from particular facts whoever proves them. Much of the English learning connected with estoppels is extremely intricate and technical, but this arises principally from two causes, the peculiarities of English special pleading, and the fact that the effect of prior judgments is usually treated by the English text writers as a branch of the law of evidence, and not as a branch of the law of Civil Procedure.

The remainder of the Act consists of a reduction to express propositions of rules as to the examination of witnesses, which are well established and understood. They call for no commentary or introduction, as they sufficiently explain their own meaning, and do not materially vary the existing law and practice.

THE

INDIAN EVIDENCE ACT

THE INDIAN EVIDENCE ACT, 1872

CONTENTS.

L

STATEMENTS BY PERSONS WHO CANNOT BE CALLED AS WITNESSES.

STATEMENTS MADE UNDER SPECIAL CIRCUMSTANCES.

HOW MUCH OF A STATEMENT IS TO BE PROVED.

JUDGMENTS OF COURT OF JUSTICE, WHEN RELEVANT.

OPINIONS OF THIRD PERSONS, WHEN RELEVANT.

CHARACTER WHEN RELEVANT.

PART II.

ON PROOF.

CHAPTER III.—FACTS WHICH NEED NOT BE PROVED.

SECTION.

56. Facts judicially noticeable need not be proved.
57. Facts of which Court must take judicial notice.
58. Facts admitted need not be proved.

CHAPTER IV.—OF ORAL EVIDENCE.

59. Proof of facts by oral evidence.
60. Oral evidence must be direct.

CHAPTER V.—OF DOCUMENTARY EVIDENCE.

61. Proof of contents of documents.
62. Primary evidence.
63. Secondary evidence.
64. Proof of documents by primary evidence.
65. Cases in which secondary evidence relating to documents may be given.
66. Rules as to notice to produce.
67. Proof of signature and handwriting of person alleged to have signed or written document produced.
68. Proof of execution of document required by law to be attested.
69. Proof where no attesting witness found.
70. Admission of execution by party to attested document.
71. Proof when attesting witness denies the execution.
72. Proof of document not required by law to be attested.
73. Comparison of signature, writing, or seal, with others admitted or proved.

PUBLIC DOCUMENTS.

74. Public documents.
75. Private documents.

PART III.

PRODUCTION AND EFFECT OF EVIDENCE.

CHAPTER VII.—OF THE BURDEN OF PROOF.

CHAPTER VIII.—ESTOPPEL.

CHAPTER IX.—OF WITNESSES.

CHAPTER X.—OF THE EXAMINATION OF WITNESSES.

ACT No. I. OF 1872.

PASSED BY THE GOVERNOR GENERAL OF INDIA IN COUNCIL.

(*Received the assent of the Governor General on the* 15*th March*, 1872).

The Indian Evidence Act, 1872.

WHEREAS it is expedient to consolidate, define, and amend the Law of Evidence: It is hereby enacted as follows:— Preamble.

PART I.

RELEVANCY OF FACTS.

CHAPTER I.—PRELIMINARY.

1. This Act may be called "The Indian Evidence Act, 1872:" Short title.

It extends to the whole of British India, and applies to all judicial proceedings in or before any Court, including Courts Martial, but not to affidavits presented to any Court or Officer, nor to proceedings before an arbitrator; Extent.

and it shall come into force on the first day of September, 1872· Commencement of Act.

2. On and from that day the following laws shall be repealed:— Repeal of enactments.

(1.) All rules of evidence not contained in any Statute, Act or Regulation in force in any part of British India:

(2.) All such rules, laws and regulations as have acquired the force of law under the twenty-fifth section of 'The Indian Councils' Act, 1861,' in so far as they relate to any matter herein provided for; and

(3.) The enactments mentioned in the schedule hereto, to the extent specified in the third column of the said schedule.

But nothing herein contained shall be deemed to affect any provision of any Statute, Act or Regulation in force in any part of British India and not hereby expressly repealed.

Interpretation-clause.

3. In this Act the following words and expressions are used in the following senses, unless a contrary intention appears from the context:

"Court."

"Court" includes all Judges and Magistrates and all persons, except arbitrators, legally authorized to take evidence.

"Fact."

"Fact" means and includes—

(1) any thing, state of things, or relation of things, capable of being perceived by the senses;

(2) any mental condition of which any person is conscious.

Illustrations.

(*a*) That there are certain objects arranged in a certain order in a certain place, is a fact.

(*b.*) That a man heard or saw something is a fact.

(*c.*) That a man said certain words is a fact.

(*d.*) That a man holds a certain opinion, has a certain intention acts in good faith, or fraudulently, or uses a particular word in a particular sense, or is or was at a specified time conscious of a particular sensation, is a fact.

(*e.*) That a man has a certain reputation is a fact.

"Relevant."

One fact is said to be relevant to another when the one is connected with the other in any of the ways referred to in the provisions of this Act relating to the relevancy of facts.

"Facts in issue."

The expression "Facts in issue" means and includes—

any fact from which, either by itself or in connection with other facts, the existence, non-existence, nature, or extent of any right, liability, or disability, asserted or denied in any suit or proceeding, necessarily follows.

Explanation.—Whenever, under the provisions of the law for the time being in force relating to Civil Procedure, any Court records an issue of fact, the fact to be asserted or denied in answer to such issue, is a fact in issue.

Illustrations.

A is accused of the murder of B.

At his trial the following facts may be in issue:—

That A caused B's death.

That A intended to cause B's death.

That A had received grave and sudden provocation from B.

That A, at the time of doing the act which caused B's death, was, by reason of unsoundness of mind, incapable of knowing its nature.

"Document" means any matter expressed or described upon any substance by means of letters, figures, or marks, or by more than one of those means, intended to be used, or which may be used, for the purpose of recording that matter. "Document."

Illustrations.

A writing is a document.

Words printed, lithographed or photographed are documents.

A map or plan is a document.

An inscription on a metal plate or stone is a document.

A caricature is a document.

"Evidence" means and includes— "Evidence."

(1) all statements which the Court permits or requires to be made before it by witnesses, in relation to matters of fact under inquiry;

such statements are called oral evidence·

(2) all documents produced for the inspection of the Court;

all such documents are called documentary evidence.

A fact is said to be proved when, after considering the matters before it, the Court either believes it to exist, or considers its existence so probable that a prudent man ought, under the circumstances of the particular case, to act upon the supposition that it exists. "Proved."

A fact is said to be disproved when, after considering the matters before it, the Court either believes that it does not exist, or considers its non-existence so probable that a prudent man ought, under the circumstances of the particular case, to act upon the supposition that it does not exist. "Disproved."

"Not proved."

A fact is said not to be proved when it is neither proved nor disproved.

"May presume."

4. Whenever it is provided by this Act that the Court may presume a fact, it may either regard such fact as proved, unless and until it is disproved, or may call for proof of it:

"Shall presume."

Whenever it is directed by this Act that the Court shall presume a fact, it shall regard such fact as proved, unless and until it is disproved:

"Conclusive proof."

When one fact is declared by this Act to be conclusive proof of another, the Court shall, on proof of the one fact, regard the other as proved, and shall not allow evidence to be given for the purpose of disproving it.

CHAPTER II.—OF THE RELEVANCY OF FACTS.

Evidence may be given of facts in issue and relevant facts.

5. Evidence may be given in any suit or proceeding of the existence or non-existence of every fact in issue and of such other facts as are hereinafter declared to be relevant, and of no others.

Explanation.—This section shall not enable any person to give evidence of a fact which he is disentitled to prove by any provision of the law for the time being in force relating to Civil Procedure.

Illustration.

(*a.*) A is tried for the murder of B by beating him with a club with the intention of causing his death.

At A's trial the following facts are in issue

A's beating B with the club.

A's causing B's death by such a beating.

A's intention to cause B's death.

(*b.*) A suitor does not bring with him, and have in readiness for production at the first hearing of the case, a bond on which he relies. This section does not enable him to produce the bond or prove its contents at a subsequent stage of the proceedings, otherwise than in accordance with the conditions prescribed by the Code of Civil Procedure.

Relevancy of facts forming

6. Facts which, though not in issue, are so connected with a fact in issue as to form part of the same transaction, are

relevant, whether they occurred at the same time and place or at different times and places.

part of same transaction.

Illustrations.

(*a.*) A is accused of the murder of B by beating him. Whatever was said or done by A or B or the by-standers at the beating, or so shortly before or after it as to form part of the transaction, is a relevant fact.

(*b.*) A is accused of waging war against the Queen by taking part in armed insurrection in which property is destroyed, troops are attacked, and gaols are broken open. The occurrence of these facts is relevant, as forming part of the general transaction, though A may not have been present at all of them.

(*c.*) A sues B for a libel contained in a letter forming part of a correspondence. Letters between the parties relating to the subject out of which the libel arose, and forming part of the correspondence it which it is contained, are relevant facts, though they do not contain the libel itself.

(*d.*) The question is, whether certain goods ordered from B were delivered to A. The goods were delivered to several intermediate persons successively. Each delivery is a relevant fact.

7. Facts which are the occasion, cause, or effect, immediate or otherwise, of relevant facts, or facts in issue, or which constitute the state of things under which they happened, or which afforded an opportunity for their occurrence or transaction, are relevant.

Facts which are occasion, cause, or effect of facts in issue.

Illustrations.

(*a.*) The question is, whether A robbed B.

The facts that, shortly before the robbery, B went to a fair with money in his possession, and that he showed it, or mentioned the fact that he had it, to third persons, are relevant.

(*b.*) The question is, whether A murdered B.

Marks on the ground, produced by a struggle at or near the place where the murder was committed, are relevant facts.

(*c.*) The question is, whether A poisoned B.

The state of B's health before the symptoms ascribed to poison, and habits of B, known to A, which afforded an opportunity for the administration of poison, are relevant facts.

Motive, preparation and previous or subsequent conduct.

8. Any fact is relevant which shows or constitutes a motive or preparation for any fact in issue or relevant fact.

The conduct of any party, or of any agent to any party, to any suit or proceeding, in reference to such suit or proceeding, or in reference to any fact in issue therein or relevant thereto, and the conduct of any person an offence against whom is the subject of any proceeding, is relevant, if such conduct influences or is influenced by any fact in issue or relevant fact, and whether it was previous or subsequent thereto.

Explanation 1.—The word "conduct" in this section does not include statements, unless those statements accompany and explain acts other than statements; but this explanation is not to affect the relevancy of statements under any other section of this Act.

Explanation 2.—When the conduct of any person is relevant, any statement made to him or in his presence and hearing, which affects such conduct, is relevant.

Illustrations.

(*a*.) A is tried for the murder of B.

The facts that A murdered C, that B knew that A had murdered C, and that B had tried to extort money from A by threatening to make his knowledge public, are relevant.

(*b*.) A sues B upon a bond for the payment of money. B denies the making of the bond.

The fact that, at the time when the bond was alleged to be made, B required money for a particular purpose, is relevant.

(*c*.) A is tried for the murder of B by poison.

The fact that, before the death of B, A procured poison similar to that which was administered to B, is relevant.

(*d*.) The question is, whether a certain document is the will of A.

The facts that, not long before the date of the alleged will, A made inquiry into matters to which the provisions of the alleged will relate; that he consulted vakils in reference to making the will, and that he caused drafts of other wills to be prepared, of which he did not approve, are relevant.

(*e*.) A is accused of a crime.

The facts that, either before, or at the time of, or after the alleged crime, A provided evidence which would tend to give to the facts of the case an appearance favourable to himself, or that he destroyed or concealed evidence, or prevented the presence or procured the absence of persons who might have been witnesses, or suborned persons to give false evidence respecting it, are relevant.

(*f.*) The question is, whether A robbed B.

The facts that, after B was robbed, C said in A's presence, 'the police are coming to look for the man who robbed B,' and that immediately afterwards A ran away, are relevant.

(*g.*) The question is, whether A owes B 10,000 rupees.

The facts that A asked C to lend him money, and that D said to C in A's presence and hearing, 'I advise you not to trust A, for he owes B 10,000 rupees, and that A went away without making any answer, are relevant facts.

(*h.*) The question is, whether A committed a crime.

The fact that A absconded after receiving a letter warning him that inquiry was being made for the criminal, and the contents of the letter, are relevant.

(*i.*) A is accused of a crime.

The facts that, after the commission of the alleged crime, he absconded, or was in possession of property or the proceeds of property acquired by the crime, or attempted to conceal things which were or might have have been used in committing it, are relevant.

(*j.*) The question is, whether A was ravished.

The facts that, shortly after the alleged rape, she made a complaint relating to the crime, the circumstances under which, and the terms in which the complaint was made, are relevant.

The fact that, without making a complaint, she said that she had been ravished is not relevant as conduct under this section, though it may be relevant

as a dying declaration under section thirty-two, clause (one), or

as corroborative evidence under section one hundred and fifty-seven.

(*k.*) The question is, whether A was robbed.

The fact that, soon after the alleged robbery, he made a complaint relating to the offence, the circumstances under which, and the terms in which, the complaint was made, are relevant.

The fact that he said he had been robbed, without making any complaint, is not relevant as conduct under this section, though it may be relevant

as a dying declaration under section thirty-two, clause (one), or as corroborative evidence under section one hundred and fifty-seven.

Facts necessary to explain or introduce relevant facts.

9. Facts necessary to explain or introduce a fact in issue or relevant fact, or which support or rebut an inference suggested by a fact in issue, or relevant fact, or which establish the identity of any thing or person whose identity is relevant, or fix the time or place at which any fact in issue or relevant fact happened, or which show the relation of parties by whom any such fact was transacted, are relevant in so far as they are necessary for that purpose.

Illustrations.

(*a.*) The question is, whether a given document is the will of A.

The state of A's property and of his family at the date of the alleged will may be relevant facts.

(*b.*) A sues B for a libel imputing disgraceful conduct to A; B affirms that the matter alleged to be libellous is true.

The position and relations of the parties at the time when the libel was published may be relevant facts as introductory to the facts in issue.

The particulars of a dispute between A and B about a matter unconnected with the alleged libel are irrelevant, though the fact that there was a dispute may be relevant if it affected the relations between A and B.

(*c.*) A is accused of a crime.

The fact that, soon after the commission of the crime, A absconded from his house, is relevant, under section eight, as conduct subsequent to and affected by facts in issue.

The fact that, at the time when he left home, he had sudden and urgent business at the place to which he went, is relevant, as tending to explain the fact that he left home suddenly.

The details of the business on which he left are not relevant, except in so far as they are necessary to show that the business was sudden and urgent.

(*d.*) A sues B for inducing C to break a contract of service made by him with A. C, on leaving A's service, says to A, 'I am leaving you because B has made me a better offer.' This statement is a relevant fact as explanatory of C's conduct, which is relevant as a fact in issue.

(*e.*) A is accused of theft, is seen to give the stolen property to B, who is seen to give it to A's wife. B says, as he delivers it, 'A says you are to hide this.' B's statement is relevant as explanatory of a fact which is part of the transaction.

(*f*.) A is tried for a riot, and is proved to have marched at the head of a mob. The cries of the mob are relevant as explanatory of the nature of the transaction.

Things said or done by conspirator in reference to common design.

10. Where there is reasonable ground to believe that two or more persons have conspired together to commit an offence or an actionable wrong, anything said, done, or written by any one of such persons in reference to their common intention, after the time when such intention was first entertained by any one of them, is a relevant fact as against each of the persons believed to be so conspiring, as well for the purpose of proving the existence of the conspiracy as for the purpose of showing that any such person was a party to it.

Illustration.

Reasonable ground exists for believing that A has joined in a conspiracy to wage war against the Queen.

The facts that B procured arms in Europe for the purpose of the conspiracy, C collected money in Calcutta for a like object, D persuaded persons to join the conspiracy in Bombay, E published writings advocating the object in view at Agra, and F transmitted from Delhi to G at Cabul the money which C had collected at Calcutta, and the contents of a letter written by H giving an account of the conspiracy, are each relevant, both to prove the existence of the conspiracy, and to prove A's complicity in it, although he may have been ignorant of all of them, and although the persons by whom they were done were strangers to him, and although they may have taken place before he joined the conspiracy or after he left it.

When facts not otherwise relevant become relevant.

11. Facts not otherwise relevant are relevant—

(1) if they are inconsistent with any fact in issue or relevant fact;

(2) if by themselves or in connection with other facts they make the existence or non-existence of any fact in issue or relevant fact highly probable or improbable.

Illustrations.

(*a.*) The question is, whether A committed a crime at Calcutta on a certain day.

The fact that, on that day, A was at Lahore is relevant.

The fact that, near the time when the crime was committed, A was at a distance from the place where it was committed, which would render it highly improbable, though not impossible, that he committed it, is relevant.

(*b.*) The question is, whether A committed a crime.

The circumstances are such that the crime must have been committed either by A, B, C, or D. Every fact which shows that the crime could have been committed by no one else, and that it was not committed by either B, C, or D, is relevant.

In suits for damages, facts tending to enable Court to determine amount are relevant.

12. In suits in which damages are claimed, any fact which will enable the Court to determine the amount of damages which ought to be awarded is relevant.

Facts relevant when right or custom is in question

13. Where the question is as to the existence of any right or custom, the following facts are relevant:—

(*a*) Any transaction by which the right or custom in question was created, claimed, modified, recognised, asserted or denied, or which was inconsistent with its existence;

(*b*) Particular instances in which the right or custom was claimed, recognised, or exercised, or in which its exercise was disputed, asserted or departed from.

Illustration.

The question is whether A has a right to a fishery. A deed conferring the fishery on A's ancestors, a mortgage of the fishery by A's father, a subsequent grant of the fishery by A's father, irreconcilable with the mortgage, particular instances in which A's father exercised the right, or in which the exercise of the right was stopped by A's neighbours, are relevant facts.

Facts showing existence of state of mind or of body or bodily feeling.

14. Facts showing the existence of any state of mind—such as intention, knowledge, good faith, negligence, rashness, ill-will or good-will towards any particular person, or showing the existence of any state of body or bodily feeling—are relevant, when the existence of any such state of mind or body or bodily feeling is in issue or relevant.

Explanation.—A fact relevant as showing the existence of a relevant state of mind must show that it exists, not generally, but in reference to the particular matter in question.

Illustrations.

(*a.*) A is accused of receiving stolen goods knowing them to be stolen. It is proved that he was in possession of a particular stolen article.

The fact that, at the same time, he was in possession of many other stolen articles is relevant, as tending to show that he knew each and all of the articles of which he was in possession to be stolen.

(*b.*) A is accused of fraudulently delivering to another person a piece of counterfeit coin which, at the time when he delivered it, he knew to be counterfeit.

The fact that at the time of its delivery, A was possessed of a number of other pieces of counterfeit coin, is relevant.

(*c.*) A sues B for damage done by a dog of B's which B knew to be ferocious.

The facts that the dog had previously bitten X, Y, and Z, and that they had made complaints to B, are relevant.

(*d.*) The question is, whether A, the accepter of a bill of exchange knew that the name of the payee was fictitious.

The fact that A had accepted other bills drawn in the same manner before they could have been transmitted to him by the payee if the payee had been a real person, is relevant, as showing that A knew that the payee was a fictitious person.

(*e.*) A is accused of defaming B by publishing an imputation intended to harm the reputation of B.

The fact of previous publications by A respecting B, showing ill-will on the part of A towards B, is relevant, as proving A's intention to harm B's reputation by the particular publication in question.

The facts that there was no previous quarrel between A and B, and that A repeated the matter complained of as he heard it, are relevant, as showing that A did not intend to harm the reputation of B.

(*f.*) A is sued by B for fraudulently representing to B that C was solvent, whereby B, being induced to trust C, who was insolvent, suffered loss.

The fact that, at the time when A represented C to be solvent, C was supposed to be solvent by his neighbours and by persons dealing with him, is relevant, as showing that A made the representation in good faith.

(*g*.) A is sued by B for the price of work done by B, upon a house of which A is owner, by the order of C, a contractor.

A's defence is that B's contract was with C.

The fact that A paid C for the work in question is relevant, as proving that A did, in good faith, make over to C the management of the work in question, so that C was in a position to contract with B on C's own account, and not as agent for A.

(*h*.) A is accused of the dishonest misappropriation of property which he had found, and the question is whether, when he appropriated it, he believed in good faith that the real owner could not be found.

The fact that public notice of the loss of the property had been given in the place where A was, is relevant, as showing that A did not in good faith believe that the real owner of the property could not be found.

The fact that A knew, or had reason to believe, that the notice was given fraudulently by C who had heard of the loss of the property and wished to set up a false claim to it, is relevant, as showing that the fact that A knew of the notice did not disprove A's good faith.

(*i*.) A is charged with shooting at B with intent to kill him. In order to show A's intent, the fact of A's having previously shot at B may be proved.

(*j*.) A is charged with sending threatening letters to B. Threatening letters previously sent by A to B may be proved, as showing the intention of the letters.

(*k*.) The question is, whether A has been guilty of cruelty towards B, his wife.

Expressions of their feeling towards each other shortly before or after the alleged cruelty, are relevant facts.

(*l*.) The question is, whether A's death was caused by poison.

Statements made by A during his illness as to his symptoms are relevant facts.

(*m*.) The question is, what was the state of A's health at the time when an assurance on his life was effected.

Statements made by A as to the state of his health at or near the time in question, are relevant facts.

(*n*.) A sues B for negligence in providing him with a carriage for hire not reasonably fit for use, whereby A was injured.

The fact that B's attention was drawn on other occasions to the defect of that particular carriage, is relevant.

The fact that B was habitually negligent about the carriages which he let to hire, is irrelevant.

(*o.*) A is tried for the murder of B by intentionally shooting him dead.

The fact that A, on other occasions, shot at B is relevant, as showing his intention to shoot B.

The fact that A was in the habit of shooting at people with intent to murder them, is irrelevant.

(*p.*) A is tried for a crime.

The fact that he said something indicating an intention to commit that particular crime, is relevant.

The fact that he said something indicating a general disposition to commit crimes of that class, is irrelevant.

Facts bearing on question whether act was accidental or intentional.

15. When there is a question whether an act was accidental or intentional, the fact that such act formed part of a series of similar occurrences, in each of which the person doing the act was concerned, is relevant.

Illustrations.

(*a.*) A is accused of burning down his house in order to obtain money for which it is insured.

The facts that A lived in several houses successively, each of which he insured, in each of which a fire occurred, and after each of which fires A received payment from a different insurance office, are relevant, as tending to show that the fires were not accidental.

(*b.*) A is employed to receive money from the debtors of B. It is A's duty to make entries in a book showing the amounts received by him. He makes an entry showing that on a particular occasion he received less than he really did receive.

The question is, whether this false entry was accidental or intentional.

The fact that other entries made by A in the same book are false, and that the false entry is in each case in favour of A, are relevant

(*c.*) A is accused of fraudulently delivering to B a counterfeit rupee.

The question is, whether the delivery of the rupee was accidental

The facts that, soon before or soon after the delivery to B, A delivered counterfeit rupees to C, D and E, are relevant, as showing that the delivery to B was not accidental.

Existence of course of business when relevant.

16. When there is a question whether a particular act was done, the existence of any course of business, according to which it naturally would have been done, is a relevant fact.

Illustrations.

(*a.*) The question is, whether a particular letter was despatched.

The facts that it was the ordinary course of business for all letters put in a certain place to be carried to the post, and that that particular letter was put into that place, are relevant.

(*b.*) The question is, whether a particular letter reached A. The facts that it was posted in due course, and was not returned through the Dead Letter Office, are relevant.

ADMISSIONS.

Admission defined.

17. An admission is a statement, oral or documentary, which suggests any inference as to any fact in issue or relevant fact, and which is made by any of the persons, and under the circumstances, hereinafter mentioned.

Admission—by party to proceeding or his agent;

18. Statements made by a party to the proceeding, or by an agent to any such party, whom the Court regards, under the circumstances of the case, as expressly or impliedly authorized by him to make them, are admissions.

by suitor in representative character:

Statements made by parties to suits, suing or sued in a representative character, are not admissions, unless they were made while the party making them held that character.

Statements made by—

by party interested in subject-by person from whom interest derived.

(1.) persons who have any proprietary or pecuniary interest in the subject-matter of the proceeding, and who make the statement in their character of persons so interested, or

(2.) persons from whom the parties to the suit have derived their interest in the subject-matter of the suit,

are admissions, if they are made during the continuance of the interest of the persons making the statements.

Admissions by persons whose position must be

19. Statements made by persons whose position or liability it is necessary to prove as against any party to the suit, are admissions, if such statements would be relevant as against such persons in relation to such position or liability in a suit

brought by or against them, and if they are made whilst the person making them occupies such position or is subject to such liability.

proved as against party to suit.

Illustration.

A undertakes to collect rents for B.

B sues A for not collecting rent due from C to B.

A denies that rent was due from C to B.

A statement by C that he owed B rent is an admission, and is a relevant fact as against A, if A denies that C did owe rent to B.

Admissions by persons expressly referred to by party to suit

20. Statements made by persons to whom a party to the suit has expressly referred for information in reference to a matter in dispute are admissions.

Illustration.

The question is, whether a horse sold by A to B is sound.

A says to B—'Go and ask C, C knows all about it.' C's statement is an admission.

Proof of admissions against persons making them, and by or on their behalf.

21. Admissions are relevant, and may be proved as against the person who makes them, or his representative in interest; but they cannot be proved by or on behalf of the person who makes them or by his representative in interest, except in the following cases:—

(1.) An admission may be proved by or on behalf of the person making it, when it is of such a nature that, if the person making it were dead, it would be relevant as between third persons under section thirty-two.

(2.) An admission may be proved by or on behalf of the person making it, when it consists of a statement of the existence of any state of mind or body, relevant or in issue, made at or about the time when such a state of mind or body existed, and is accompanied by conduct rendering its falsehood improbable.

(3.) An admission may be proved by or on behalf of the person making it, if it is relevant otherwise than as an admission.

Illustrations.

(*a.*) The question between A and B is, whether a certain deed is or is not forged. A affirms that it is genuine, B that it is forged.

A may prove a statement by B that the deed is genuine, and B may prove a statement by A that the deed is forged; but A cannot prove a statement by himself that the deed is genuine, nor can B prove a statement by himself that the deed is forged.

(*b.*) A, the captain of a ship, is tried for casting her away.

Evidence is given to show that the ship was taken out of her proper course.

A produces a book kept by him in the ordinary course of his business, showing observations alleged to have been taken by him from day to day, and indicating that the ship was not taken out of her proper course. A may prove these statements, because they would be admissible between third parties, if he were dead, under section thirty-two, clause (two).

(*c.*) A is accused of a crime committed by him at Calcutta.

He produces a letter written by himself and dated at Lahore on that day, and bearing the Lahore post-mark of that day.

The statement in the date of the letter is admissible, because, if A were dead, it would be admissible under section thirty-two, clause (two.)

(*d.*) A is accused of receiving stolen goods knowing them to be stolen.

He offers to prove that he refused to sell them below their value.

A may prove these statements, though they are admissions, because they are explanatory of conduct influenced by facts in issue.

(*e.*) A is accused of fraudulently having in his possession counterfeit coin which he knew to be counterfeit.

He offers to prove that he asked a skilful person to examine the coin, as he doubted whether it was counterfeit or not, and that that person did examine it and told him it was genuine.

A may prove these facts for the reasons stated in the last preceding illustration.

When oral admissions as to contents of

22. Oral admissions as to the contents of a document are not relevant, unless and until the party proposing to prove them shows that he is entitled to give secondary evidence of

the contents of such document under the rules hereinafter contained, or unless the genuineness of a document produced is in question.

documents are relevant.

Admissions in civil cases, when relevant.

23. In civil cases no admission is relevant, if it is made either upon an express condition that evidence of it is not to be given, or under circumstances from which the Court can infer that the parties agreed together that evidence of it should not be given.

Explanation.—Nothing in this section shall be taken to exempt any barrister, pleader, attorney or vakil from giving evidence of any matter of which he may be compelled to give evidence under section one hundred and twenty-six.

Confession caused by inducement, threat or promise when irrelevant in criminal proceeding.

24. A confession made by an accused person is irrelevant in a criminal proceeding, if the making of the confession appears to the Court to have been caused by any inducement, threat or promise, having reference to the charge against the accused person, proceeding from a person in authority and sufficient, in the opinion of the Court, to give the accused person grounds, which would appear to him reasonable, for supposing that by making it he would gain any advantage or avoid any evil of a temporal nature in reference to the proceedings against him.

Confession to Police officer not to be proved.

25. No confession made to a Police officer, shall be proved as against a person accused of any offence.

Confession by accused while in custody of Police not to be proved against him.

26. No confession made by any person whilst he is in the custody of a Police officer, unless it be made in the immediate presence of a Magistrate, shall be proved as against such person.

How much of information received from accused may be proved.

27. Provided that, when any fact is deposed to as discovered in consequence of information received from a person accused of any offence, in the custody of a Police officer, so much of such information, whether it amounts to a confession or not, as relates distinctly to the fact thereby discovered, may be proved.

Confession made after removal of

28. If such a confession as is referred to in section twenty-four is made after the impression caused by any such induce-

impression caused by inducement, threat, or promise, relevant.

ment, threat or promise has, in the opinion of the Court, been fully removed, it is relevant.

Confession otherwise relevant not to become irrelevant because of promise of secrecy, &c.

29. If such a confession is otherwise relevant, it does not become irrelevant merely because it was made under a promise of secrecy, or in consequence of a deception practised on the accused person for the purpose of obtaining it, or when he was drunk, or because it was made in answer to questions which he need not have answered, whatever may have been the form of those questions, or because he was not warned that he was not bound to make such confession, and that evidence of it might be given against him.

Consideration of proved confession affecting person making it and others jointly under trial for same offence.

30. When more persons than one are being tried jointly for the same offence, and a confession made by one of such persons affecting himself and some other of such persons is proved, the Court may take into consideration such confession as against such other person as well as against the person who makes such confession.

Illustrations.

(*a*.) A and B are jointly tried for the murder of C. It is proved that A said,—'B and I murdered C.' The Court may consider the effect of this confession as against B.

(*b*.) A is on his trial for the murder of C. There is evidence to show that C was murdered by A and B, and that B said,—'A and I murdered C.'

This statement may not be taken into consideration by the Court against A, as B is not being jointly tried.

Admissions not conclusive proof, but may estop.

31. Admissions are not conclusive proof of the matters admitted, but they may operate as estoppels under the provisions hereinafter contained.

Statements by Persons who cannot be called as Witnesses.

Cases in which statement of relevant fact by person who is

32. Statements, written or verbal, of relevant facts made by a person who is dead, or who cannot be found, or who has become incapable of giving evidence, or whose attendance cannot be procured without an amount of delay or expense

hich, under the circumstances of the case, appears to the ourt unreasonable, are themselves relevant facts in the ollowing cases :—

dead or cannot be found, &c. is relevant.

(1) When the statement is made by a person as to the ause of his death, or as to any of the circumstances of the ransaction which resulted in his death, in cases in which the ause of that person's death comes into question.

When it relates to cause of death;

Such statements are relevant whether the person who made hem was or was not, at the time when they were made, ınder expectation of death, and whatever may be the nature of the proceeding in which the cause of his death comes into question.

(2) When the statement was made by such person in the ordinary course of business, and in particular when it consists of any entry or memorandum made by him in books kept in the ordinary course of business, or in the discharge of professional duty; or of an acknowledgment written or signed by him of the receipt of money, goods, securities or property of any kind; or of a document used in commerce written or signed by him, or of the date of a letter or other document usually dated, written or signed by him.

or is made in course of business;

(3) When the statement is against the pecuniary or proprietary interest of the person making it, or when, if true, it would expose him or would have exposed him to a criminal prosecution or to a suit for damages.

or against interest of maker;

(4) When the statement gives the opinion of any such person, as to the existence of any public right or custom or matter of public or general interest, of the existence of which, if it existed, he would have been likely to be aware, and when such statmeent was made before any controversy as to such right, custom or matter had arisen.

or gives opinion as to public right or custom, or matters of general interest;

(5) When the statement relates to the existence of any relationship + between persons as to whose relationship + the person making the statement had special means of knowledge, and when the statement was made before the question in dispute was raised.

or relates to existence of relationship; by blood, or adoption or is made in will or deed relating to family affairs;

(6) When the statement relates to the existence of any relationship between persons deceased, and is made in any will or deed relating to the affairs of the family to which any such deceased person belonged or in any family pedigree, or upon any tombstone, family portrait or other thing on which such statements are usually made, and when such statement was made before the question in dispute was raised.

or in document relating to transaction mentioned in section 13, clause (*a*);

(7). When the statement is contained in any deed, will or other document which relates to any such transaction as is mentioned in section thirteen, clause (*a*).

or is made by several persons and expresses feeling relevant to matter in question.

(8) When the statement was made by a number of persons and expressed feelings or impressions on their part relevant to the matter in question.

Illustrations.

(*a.*) The question is, whether A was murdered by B; or

A dies of injuries received in a transaction in the course of which she was ravished. The question is, whether she was ravished by B; or

The question is, whether A was killed by B under such circumstances that a suit would lie against B by A's widow.

Statements made by A as to the cause of his or her death, referring respectively to the murder, the rape, and the actionable wrong under consideration, are relevant facts.

(*b.*) The question is as to the date of A's birth.

An entry in the diary of a deceased surgeon, regularly kept in the course of business, stating that, on a given day, he attended A's mother and delivered her of a son, is a relevant fact.

(*c.*) The question is, whether A was in Calcutta on a given day.

A statement in the diary of a deceased solicitor, regularly kept in the course of business, that, on a given day, the solicitor attended A at a place mentioned, in Calcutta, for the purpose of conferring with him upon specified business, is a relevant fact.

(*d.*) The question is, whether a ship sailed from Bombay harbour on a given day.

A letter written by a deceased member of a merchant's firm, by which she was chartered, to their correspondents in London to whom the cargo was consigned, stating that the ship sailed on a given day from Bombay harbour, is a relevant fact.

(*e.*) The question is, whether rent was paid to A for certain land.

A letter from A's deceased agent to A, saying that he had received the rent on A's account, and held it at A's orders, is a relevant fact.

(*f.*) The question is whether A and B were legally married.

The statement of a deceased clergyman that he married them under such circumstances that the celebration would be a crime, is relevant.

(*g.*) The question is, whether A, a person who cannot be found, wrote a letter on a certain day. The fact that a letter written by him is dated on that day, is relevant.

(*h.*) The question is, what was the cause of the wreck of a ship.

A protest made by the captain, whose attendance cannot be procured, is a relevant fact.

(*i.*) The question is, whether a given road is a public way.

A statement by A, a deceased headman of the village, that the road was public, is a relevant fact.

(*j.*) The question is, what was the price of grain on a certain day in a particular market. A statement of the price, made by a deceased banya in the ordinary course of his business, is a relevant fact.

(*k.*) The question is, whether A, who is dead, was the father of B.

A statement by A that B was his son, is a relevant fact.

(*l.*) The question is, what was the date of the birth of A.

A letter from A's deceased father to a friend, announcing the birth of A on a given day, is a relevant fact.

(*m.*) The question is, whether, and when, A and B were married.

An entry in a memorandum-book by C, the deceased father of B, of his daughter's marriage with A on a given date, is a relevant fact.

(*n.*) A sues B for a libel expressed in a painted caricature exposed in a shop window. The question is as to the similarity of the caricature and its libellous character. The remarks of a crowd of spectators on these points may be proved.

Relevancy of certain evidence for proving, in subsequent proceeding, the truth of facts therein stated.

33. Evidence given by a witness in a judicial proceeding, or before any person authorized by law to take it, is relevant for the purpose of proving, in a subsequent judicial proceeding, or in a later stage of the same judicial proceeding, the truth of the facts which it states, when the witness is dead or cannot be found, or is incapable of giving evidence, or is kept out of the way by the adverse party, or if his presence cannot be obtained without an amount of delay or expense

which, under the circumstances of the case, the court considers unreasonable.

Provided—

that the proceeding was between the same parties or their representatives in interest:

that the adverse party in the first proceeding had the right and opportunity to cross-examine;

that the questions in issue were substantially the same in the first as in the second proceeding.

Explanation.—A criminal trial or inquiry shall be deemed to be a proceeding between the prosecutor and the accused within the meaning of this section.

STATEMENTS MADE UNDER SPECIAL CIRCUMSTANCES.

Entries in books of account when relevant.

34. Entries in books of account, regularly kept in the course of business, are relevant whenever they refer to a matter into which the Court has to inquire, but such statements shall not alone be sufficient evidence to charge any person with liability.

Illustration.

A sues B for Rs. 1,000, and shows entries in the account-books showing B to be indebted to him to this amount. The entries are relevant, but are not sufficient, without other evidence, to prove the debt.

Relevancy of entry in public record, made in performance of duty.

35. An entry in any public or other official book, register, or record, stating a fact in issue or relevant fact, and made by a public servant in the discharge of his official duty, or by any other person in performance of a duty specially enjoined by the law of the country in which such book, register, or record is kept, is itself a relevant fact.

Relevancy of statements in maps, charts and plans.

36. Statements of facts in issue or relevant facts, made in published maps or charts generally offered for public sale, or in maps or plans made under the authority of Government, as to matters usually represented or stated in such maps, charts, or plans, are themselves relevant facts.

37. When the Court has to form an opinion as to the

existence of any fact of a public nature, any statement of it, made in a recital contained in any Act of Parliament, or in any Act of the Governor General of India in Council, or of the Governors in Council of Madras or Bombay, or of the Lieutenant-Governor in Council of Bengal, or in a notification of the Government appearing in the *Gazette of India*, or in the Gazette of any Local Government, or in any printed paper purporting to be the *London Gazette* or the *Government Gazette* of any colony or possession of the Queen, is a relevant fact.

Relevancy of statement as to fact of public nature, contained in certain Acts or notifications.

38. When the Court has to form an opinion as to a law of any country, any statement of such law contained in a book purporting to be printed or published under the authority of the Government of such country and to contain any such law, and any report of a ruling of the Courts of such country contained in a book purporting to be a report of such rulings, is relevant.

Relevancy of statements as to any law contained in law books.

How much of a Statement is to be proved.

39. When any statement of which evidence is given forms part of a longer statement, or of a conversation or part of an isolated document, or is contained in a document which forms part of a book, or of a connected series of letters or papers, evidence shall be given of so much and no more of the statement, conversation, document, book, or series of letters or papers as the Court considers necessary in that particular case to the full understanding of the nature and effect of the statement, and of the circumstances under which it was made.

What evidence to be given when statement forms part of a conversation, document, book, or series of letters or papers.

Judgments of Courts of Justice, when relevant.

40. The existence of any judgment, order or decree which by law prevents any Court from taking cognizance of a suit or holding a trial, is a relevant fact when the question is whether such Court ought to take cognizance of such suit, or to hold such trial.

Previous judgments relevant to bar a second suit for trial.

41. A final judgment, order or decree of a competent

Relevancy of certain

judgments in probate, &c., jurisdiction.

Court, in the exercise of probate, matrimonial, admiralty or insolvency jurisdiction, which confers upon or takes away from any person any legal character, or which declares any person to be entitled to any such character, or to be entitled to any specific thing, not as against any specified person but absolutely, is relevant when the existence of any such legal character, or the title of any such person to any such thing, is relevant.

Such judgment, order or decree is conclusive proof

that any legal character, which it confers accrued at the time when such judgment, order or decree came into operation;

that any legal character, to which it declares any such person to be entitled, accrued to that person at the time when such judgment declares it to have accrued to that person;

that any legal character which it takes away from any such person ceased at the time from which such judgment declared that it had ceased or should cease;

and that any thing to which it declares any person to be so entitled was the property of that person at the time from which such judgment declares that it had been or should be his property.

Relevancy and effect of judgments orders or decrees, other than those mentioned in section 41.

42. Judgments, orders or decrees other than those mentioned in section forty-one, are relevant if they relate to matters of a public nature relevant to the enquiry; but such judgments, orders or decrees are not conclusive proof of that which they state.

Illustration.

A sues B for trespass on his land. B alleges the existence of a public right of way over the land, which A denies.

The existence of a decree in favour of the defendant, in a suit by A against C for a trespass on the same land, in which C alleged the existence of the same right of way, is relevant, but it is not conclusive proof that the right of way exists.

Judgments &c., other than

43. Judgments, orders or decrees, other than those mentioned in sections forty, forty-one and forty-two, are

irrelevant, unless the existence of such judgment, order or decree, is a fact in issue, or is relevant under some other provision of this Act.

those mentioned in sections 40-42, when relevant.

Illustrations.

(*a.*) A and B separately sue C for a libel which reflects upon each of them. C in each case says, that the matter alleged to be libellous is true, and the circumstances are such that it is probably true in each case, or in neither.

A obtains a decree against C for damages on the ground that C failed to make out his justification. The fact is irrelevant as between B and C.

(*b.*) A prosecutes B, for adultery, with C, A's wife.

B denies that C is A's wife, but the court convicts B of adultery.

Afterwards C is prosecuted for bigamy in marrying B during A's lifetime. C says that she never was A's wife.

The judgment against B is irrelevant as against C.

(*c.*) A prosecutes B for stealing a cow from him. B is convicted.

A, afterwards, sues C for the cow, which B had sold to him before his conviction. As between A and C, the judgment against B is irrelevant.

(*d.*) A has obtained a decree for the possession of land against B C, B's son, murders A in consequence.

The existence of the judgment is relevant, as showing motive for a crime.

44. Any party to a suit or other proceeding may show that any judgment, order or decree which is relevant under section forty, forty-one or forty-two, and which has been proved by the adverse party, was delivered by a Court not competent to deliver it, or was obtained by fraud or collusion.

Fraud or collusion in obtaining judgment, or incompetency of Court, may be proved.

OPINIONS OF THIRD PERSONS, WHEN RELEVANT.

45. When the Court has to form an opinion upon a point of foreign law, or of science or art, or as to identity of handwriting, the opinions upon that point of persons specially skilled in such foreign law, science or art, are relevant facts.

Opinions of experts.

Such persons are called experts.

Illustrations.

(*a.*) The question is, whether the death of A was caused by poison.

The opinions of experts as to the symptoms produced by the poison by which A is supposed to have died, are relevant.

(*b.*) The question is, whether A, at the time of doing a certain act, was, by reason of unsoundness of mind, incapable of knowing the nature of the act, or that he was doing what was either wrong or contrary to law.

The opinions of experts upon the question whether the symptoms exhibited by A commonly show unsoundness of mind, and whether such unsoundness of mind usually renders persons incapable of knowing the nature of the acts which they do, or of knowing that what they do is either wrong or contrary to law, are relevant.

(*c.*) The question is, whether a certain document was written by A. Another document is produced which is proved or admitted to have been written by A.

The opinion of experts on the question whether the two documents were written by the same person or by different persons, are relevant.

Facts bearing upon opinions of experts.

46. Facts, not otherwise relevant, are relevant if they support or are inconsistent with the opinions of experts, when such opinions are relevant.

Illustrations.

(*a*) The question is, whether A was poisoned by a certain poison.

The fact that other persons, who were poisoned by that poison, exhibited certain symptoms which experts affirm or deny to be the symptoms of that poison, is relevant.

(*b.*) The question is, whether an obstruction to a harbour is caused by a certain sea-wall.

The fact that other harbours similarly situated in other respects, but where there were no such sea-walls, began to be obstructed at about the same time is relevant.

Opinion as to handwriting, when relevant.

47. When the Court has to form an opinion as to the person by whom any document was written or signed, the opinion of any person acquainted with the handwriting of the person by whom it is supposed to be written or signed that it was or was not written or signed by that person, is a relevant fact.

Explanation.—A person is said to be acquainted with the handwriting of another person when he has seen that person write, or when he has received documents purporting to be written by that person in answer to documents written by himself or under his authority and addressed to that person, or when, in the ordinary course of business, documents purporting to be written by that person have been habitually submitted to him.

Illustration.

The question is, whether a given letter is in the handwriting of A, a merchant in London.

B is a merchant in Calcutta, who has written letters addressed to A and received letters purporting to be written by him. C is B's clerk, whose duty it was to examine and file B's correspondence. D is B's broker, to whom B habitually submitted the letters purporting to be written by A for the purpose of advising with him thereon.

The opinions of B, C and D on the question whether the letter is in the handwriting of A are relevant, though neither B, C nor D ever saw A write.

Opinion as to existence of right or custom, when relevant.

48. When the Court has to form an opinion as to the existence of any general custom or right, the opinions, as to the existence of such custom or right, of persons who would be likely to know of its existence if it existed, are relevant.

Explanation.—The expression 'general custom or right' includes customs or rights common to any considerable class of persons.

Illustration.

The right of the villagers of a particular village to use the water of a particular well is a general right within the meaning of this section.

Opinions as to usages, tenets, &c., when relevant.

49. When the Court has to form an opinion as to—

the usages and tenets of any body of men or family,

the constitution and government of any religious or charitable foundation, or

the meaning of words or terms used in particular districts or by particular classes of people,

the opinions of persons having special means of knowledge thereon, are relevant facts.

Opinion on relationship,

50. When the Court has to form an opinion as to the relationship of one person to another, the opinion, expressed

when relevant.

by conduct, as to the existence of such relationship, of any person who, as a member of the family or otherwise, has special means of knowledge on the subject, is a relevant fact: Provided that such opinion shall not be sufficient to prove a marriage in proceedings under the Indian Divorce Act, or in prosecutions under section four hundred and ninety-four, four hundred and ninety-five, four hundred and ninety-seven or four hundred and ninety-eight of the Indian Penal Code.

Illustrations.

(*a.*) The question is, whether A and B were married.

The fact that they were usually received and treated by their friends as married persons, is relevant.

(*b.*) The question is, whether A was the legitimate son of B. The fact that A was always treated as such by the members of the family, is relevant.

Grounds of opinion when relevant.

51. Whenever the opinion of any living person is relevant, the grounds on which such opinion is based are also relevant.

Illustration.

An expert may give an account of experiments performed by him for the purpose of forming his opinion.

CHARACTER WHEN RELEVANT.

In civil cases character to prove conduct imputed, irrelevant.

52. In civil cases, the fact that the character of any person concerned is such as to render probable or improbable any conduct imputed to him, is irrelevant, except in so far as such character appears from facts otherwise relevant.

In criminal cases, previous good character relevant.

53. In criminal proceedings, the fact that the person accused is of good character, is relevant.

In criminal proceedings previous conviction relevant, but not previous bad character, except in reply.

54. In criminal proceedings, the fact that the accused person has been previously convicted of any offence is relevant; but the fact that he has a bad character is irrelevant, unless evidence has been given that he has a good character, in which case it becomes relevant.

Explanation.—This section does not apply to cases in which the bad character of any person is itself a fact in issue.

55. In civil cases, the fact that the character of any person is such as to affect the amount of damages which he ought to receive, is relevant. Character as affecting damages.

Explanation.—In sections fifty-two, fifty-three, fifty-four and fifty-five, the word 'character' includes both reputation and disposition; but evidence may be given only of general reputation and general disposition, and not of particular acts by which reputation or disposition were shown.

PART II.

ON PROOF.

CHAPTER III.—FACTS WHICH NEED NOT BE PROVED.

Facts judicially noticeable need not be proved.

56. No fact of which the Court will take judicial notice need be proved.

Facts of which Court must take judicial notice.

57. The Court shall take judicial notice of the following facts :—

(1.) All laws or rules having the force of law now or heretofore in force, or hereafter to be in force, in any part of British India :

(2.) All public Acts passed or hereafter to be passed by Parliament, and all local and personal Acts directed by Parliament to be judicially noticed :

(3.) Articles of War for Her Majesty's Army or Navy :

(4.) The course of proceeding of Parliament and of the Councils for the purposes of making Laws and Regulations established under the Indian Councils' Act, or any other law for the time being relating thereto :

Explanation.—The word ' Parliament,' in clauses (two) and (four), includes—

1. The Parliament of the United Kingdom of Great Britain and Ireland ;
2. The Parliament of Great Britain ;
3. The Parliament of England ;
4. The Parliament of Scotland, and
5. The Parliament of Ireland :

(5.) The accession and the sign manual of the Sovereign

for the time being of the United Kingdom of Great Britain and Ireland:

(6.) All seals of which English Courts take judicial notice: the seals of all the Courts of British India, and of all Courts out of British India, established by the authority of the Governor General or any Local Government in Council: the seals of Courts of Admiralty and Maritime Jurisdiction and of Notaries Public, and all seals which any person is authorized to use by any Act of Parliament or other Act or Regulation having the force of law in British India:

(7.) The accession to office, names, titles, functions, and signatures of the persons filling for the time being any public office in any part of British India, if the fact of the appointment to such office is notified in the *Gazette of India*, or in the official Gazette of any Local Government:

(8.) The existence, title, and national flag of every State or Sovereign recognised by the British Crown:

(9.) The divisions of time, the geographical divisions of the world, and public festivals, fasts and holidays notified in the official Gazette:

(10.) The territories under the dominion of the British Crown:

(11.) The commencement, continuance, and termination of hostilities between the British Crown and any other State or body of persons:

(12.) The names of the members and officers of the Court and of their deputies and subordinate officers and assistants, and also of all officers acting in execution of its process, and of all advocates, attornies, proctors, vakīls, pleaders and other persons authorized by law to appear or act before it:

(13.) The rule of the road. on land or at sea

In all these cases, and also in all matters of public history, literature, science or art, the Court may resort for its aid to appropriate books or documents of reference.

If the Court is called upon by any person to take judicial notice of any fact, it may refuse to do so, unless and until such person produces any such book or document as it may consider necessary to enable it to do so.

Facts admitted need not be proved.

58. No fact need be proved in any proceeding which the parties thereto or their agents agree to admit at the hearing, or which, before the hearing, they agree to admit by any writing under their hands, or which by any rule of pleading in force at the time they are deemed to have admitted by their pleadings: Provided that the Court may, in its discretion, require the facts admitted to be proved otherwise than by such admissions.

CHAPTER IV.—OF ORAL EVIDENCE.

Proof of facts by oral evidence.

59. All facts, except the contents of documents, may be proved by oral evidence.

Oral evidence must be direct.

60. Oral evidence must, in all cases, whatever, be direct; That is to say—

If it refers to a fact which could be seen, it must be the evidence of a witness who says he saw it;

If it refers to a fact which could be heard, it must be the evidence of a witness who says he heard it;

If it refers to a fact which could be perceived by any other sense or in any other manner, it must be the evidence of a witness who says he perceived it by that sense or in that manner;

If it refers to an opinion or to the grounds on which that opinion is held, it must be the evidence of the person who holds that opinion on those grounds:

Provided that the opinions of experts expressed in any treatise commonly offered for sale, and the grounds on which such opinions are held, may be proved by the production of such treatises if the author is dead or cannot be found, or has become incapable of giving evidence, or cannot be called as a witness without an amount of delay or expense which the Court regards as unreasonable:

Provided also, that, if oral evidence refers to the existence or condition of any material thing other than a document, the

Court may, if it thinks fit, require the production of such material thing for its inspection.

CHAPTER V.—OF DOCUMENTARY EVIDENCE.

61. The contents of documents may be proved either by primary or by secondary evidence.

Proof of contents of documents.

62. Primary evidence means the document itself produced for the inspection of the Court.

Primary evidence.

Explanation 1.—Where a document is executed in several parts, each part is primary evidence of the document:

Where a document is executed in counterpart, each counterpart being executed by one or some of the parties only, each counterpart is primary evidence as against the parties executing it.

Explanation 2.—Where a number of documents are all made by one uniform process, as in the case of printing, lithography, or photography, each is primary evidence of the contents of the rest; but where they are all copies of a common original, they are not primary evidence of the contents of the original.

Illustration.

A person is shown to have been in possession of a number of placards, all printed at one time from one original. Any one of the placards is primary evidence of the contents of any other, but no one of them is primary evidence of the contents of the original.

63. Secondary evidence means and includes—

Secondary evidence.

(1.) Certified copies given under the provisions hereinafter contained;

(2.) Copies made from the original by mechanical processes which in themselves insure the accuracy of the copy, and copies compared with such copies;

(3.) Copies made from or compared with the original;

(4.) Counterparts of documents as against the parties who did not execute them;

(5.) Oral accounts of the contents of a document given by some person who has himself seen it.

Illustrations.

(*a.*) A photograph of an original is secondary evidence of its contents, though the two have not been compared, if it is proved that the thing photographed was the original.

(*b.*) A copy compared with a copy of a letter made by a copying machine is secondary evidence of the contents of the letter, if it be shown that the copy made by the machine was made from the original.

(*c.*) A copy transcribed from a copy, but afterwards compared with the original, is secondary evidence; but the copy not so compared is not secondary evidence of the original, although the copy from which it was transcribed was compared with the original.

(*d.*) Neither an oral account of a copy compared with the original, nor an oral account of a photograph or machine-copy of the original, is secondary evidence of the original.

Proof of documents by primary evidence.

64. Documents must be proved by primary evidence except in the cases hereinafter mentioned.

Cases in which secondary evidence relating to documents may be given.

65. Secondary evidence may be given of the existence, condition, or contents of a document in the following cases:—

(*a.*) When the original is shown or appears to be in the possession or power

of the person against whom the document is sought to be proved, or

of any person out of reach of, or not subject to, the process of the Court, or

of any person legally bound to produce it,

and when, after the notice mentioned in section sixty-six, such person does not produce it;

(*b.*) When the existence, condition or contents of the original have been proved to be admitted in writing by the person against whom it is proved or by his representative in interest;

(*c.*) When the original has been destroyed or lost, or when the party offering evidence of its contents cannot, for any other reason not arising from his own default or neglect, produce it in reasonable time;

(*d.*) When the original is of such a nature as not to be easily moveable;

(*e.*) When the original is a public document within the meaning of section seventy-four;

(*f.*) When the original is a document of which a certified copy is permitted by this Act, or by any other law in force in British India, to be given in evidence;

(*g.*) When the originals consist of numerous accounts or other documents which cannot conveniently be examined in Court, and the fact to be proved is the general result of the whole collection.

In cases (*a.*), (*c.*) and (*d.*), any secondary evidence of the contents of the document is admissible.

In case (*b.*), the written admission is admissible.

In case (*e.*) or (*f.*) a certified copy of the document, but no other kind of secondary evidence is admissible.

In case (*g.*), evidence may be given as to the general result of the documents by any person who has examined them, and who is skilled in the examination of such documents.

Rules as to notice to produce.

66. Secondary evidence of the contents of the documents referred to in section sixty-five, clause (*a.*), shall not be given unless the party proposing to give such secondary evidence has previously given to the party in whose possession or power the document is, such notice to produce it as is prescribed by law; and if no notice is prescribed by law, then such notice as the Court considers reasonable under the circumstances of the case:

Provided that such notice shall not be required in order to render secondary evidence admissible in any of the following cases, or in any other case in which the Court thinks fit to dispense with it:—

(1.) When the document to be proved is itself a notice;

(2.) When, from the nature of the case, the adverse party must know that he will be required to produce it;

(3.) When it appears or is proved that the adverse party has obtained possession of the original by fraud or force;

(4.) When the adverse party or his agent has the original in Court;

(5.) When the adverse party or his agent has admitted the loss of the document;

(6.) When the person in possession of the document is out of reach of, or not subject to, the process of the Court.

Proof of signature and handwriting of person alleged to have signed or written document produced.

67. If a document is alleged to be signed or to have been written wholly or in part by any person, the signature or the handwriting of so much of the document as is alleged to be in that person's handwriting must be proved to be in his handwriting.

Proof of execution of document required by law to be attested.

68. If a document is required by law to be attested, it shall not be used as evidence until one attesting witness at least has been called for the purpose of proving its execution, if there be an attesting witness alive, and subject to the process of the Court and capable of giving evidence.

Proof where no attesting witness found.

69. If no such attesting witness can be found, or if the document purports to have been executed in the United Kingdom, it must be proved that the attestation of one attesting witness at least is in his handwriting, and that the signature of the person executing the document is in the handwriting of that person.

Admission of execution by party to attested document.

70. The admission of a party to an attested document of its execution by himself shall be sufficient proof of its execution as against him, though it be a document required by law to be attested.

Proof when attesting witness denies the execution.

71. If the attesting witness denies or does not recollect the execution of the document, its execution may be proved by other evidence.

Proof of document not required by law to be attested.

72. An attested document not required by law to be attested may be proved as if it was unattested.

Comparison of

73. In order to ascertain whether a signature, writing, or seal is that of the person by whom it purports to have been written or made, any signature, writing, or seal admitted or

proved to the satisfaction of the Court to have been written or made by that person may be compared with the one which is to be proved, although that signature, writing, or seal has not been produced or proved for any other purpose.

signature, writing or seal with others admitted or proved.

The Court may direct any person present in Court to write any words or figures for the purpose of enabling the Court to compare the words or figures so written with any words or figures alleged to have been written by such person.

PUBLIC DOCUMENTS.

Public documents.

74. The following documents are public documents:—

1. Documents forming the acts or records of the acts,

(i.) of the sovereign authority,

(ii.) of official bodies and tribunals, and

(iii.) of public officers, legislative, judicial, and executive, whether of British India, or of any other part of Her Majesty's dominions, or of a foreign country.

2. Public records kept in India of private documents.

Private documents.

75. All other documents are private.

Certified copies of public documents.

76. Every public officer having the custody of a public document which any person has a right to inspect, shall give that person on demand a copy of it on payment of the legal fees therefor, together with a certificate written at the foot of such copy that it is a true copy of such document or part thereof, as the case may be, and such certificate shall be dated and subscribed by such officer with his name and his official title, and shall be sealed, whenever such officer is authorized by law to make use of a seal; and such copies so certified shall be called certified copies.

Explanation.—Any officer who, by the exercise of official duty, is authorized to deliver such copies, shall be deemed to have the custody of such documents within the meaning of this section.

Proof of documents by production of certified copies.

77. Such certified copies may be produced in proof of the contents of the public documents or parts of the public documents of which they purport to be copies.

Proof of other official documents.

78. The following public documents may be proved as follows :—

(1.) Acts, orders or notifications of the Executive Government of British India in any of its departments, or of any Local Government or any department of any Local Government,

by the records of the departments, certified by the heads of those departments respectively,

or by any document purporting to be printed by order of any such Government :

(2.) The proceedings of the Legislatures,

by the journals of those bodies respectively, or by published Acts or abstracts, or by copies purporting to be printed by order of Government :

(3.) Proclamations, orders or regulations issued by Her Majesty or by the Privy Council, or by any department of Her Majesty's Government,

by copies or extracts contained in the *London Gazette*, or purporting to be printed by the Queen's printer :

(4.) The acts of the Executive or the proceedings of the legislature of a foreign country,

by journals published by their authority, or commonly received in that country as such, or by a copy certified under the seal of the country or sovereign, or by a recognition thereof in some public Act of the Governor General of India, in Council :

(5.) The proceedings of a municipal body in British India,

by a copy of such proceedings, certified by the legal keeper thereof, or by a printed book purporting to be published by the authority of such body ·

(6.) Public documents of any other class in a foreign country,

by the original, or by a copy certified by the legal keeper thereof, with a certificate under the seal of a Notary Public, or of a British Consul or diplomatic agent, that the copy is duly certified by the officer having the legal custody of the original, and upon proof of the character of the document according to the law of the foreign country.

PRESUMPTIONS AS TO DOCUMENTS.

79. The Court shall presume every document purporting to be a certificate, certified copy, or other document, which is by law declared to be admissible as evidence of any particular fact, and which purports to be duly certified by any officer in British India, or by any officer in any Native State in alliance with Her Majesty, who is duly authorized thereto by the Governor General in Council, to be genuine: Provided that such document is substantially in the form and purports to be executed in the manner directed by law in that behalf.

Presumption as to genuineness of certified copies.

The Court shall also presume that any officer by whom any such document purports to be signed or certified held, when he signed it, the official character which he claims in such paper.

80. Whenever any document is produced before any Court, purporting to be a record or memorandum of the evidence, or of any part of the evidence, given by a witness in a judicial proceeding or before any officer authorized by law to take such evidence, or to be a statement or confession by any prisoner or accused person, taken in accordance with law, and purporting to be signed by any Judge or Magistrate, or by such officer as aforesaid, the Court shall presume—

Presumption as to documents produced as record of evidence.

that the document is genuine; that any statements as to the circumstances under which it was taken, purporting to be made by the person signing it, are true, and that such evidence, statement or confession was duly taken.

81. The Court shall presume the genuineness of every document purporting to be the *London Gazette*, or the *Gazette of India*, or the Government Gazette of any Local Government, or of any colony, dependency, or possession of the British Crown, or to be a newspaper or a journal, or to be copy of a private Act of Parliament printed by the Queen's Printer, and of every document purporting to be a document

Presumption as to Gazettes, newspapers, private Acts of Parliament, and other documents.

directed by any law to be kept by any person, if such document is kept substantially in the form required by law and is produced from proper custody.

Presumption as to document admissible in England without proof of seal or signature.

82. When any document is produced before any Court, purporting to be a document which, by the law in force for the time being in England or Ireland, would be admissible in proof of any particular in any Court of Justice in England or Ireland, without proof of the seal, or stamp or signature authenticating it, or of the judicial or official character claimed by the person by whom it purports to be signed, the Court shall presume that such seal, stamp or signature is genuine, and that the person signing it held, at the time when he signed it, the judicial or official character which he claims,

and the document shall be admissible for the same purpose for which it would be admissible in England or Ireland.

Presumption as to maps or plans made by authority of Government.

83. The Court shall presume that maps or plans purporting to be made by the authority of Government were so made, and are accurate; but maps or plans made for the purposes of any cause must be proved to be accurate.

Presumption as to collections of laws and reports of decisions.

84. The Court shall presume the genuineness of every book purporting to be printed or published under the authority of the Government of any country, and to contain any of the laws of that country,

and of every book purporting to contain reports of decisions of the Courts of such country.

Presumption as to powers-of-attorney.

85. The Court shall presume that every document purporting to be a power-of-attorney, and to have been executed before, and authenticated by, a Notary Public, or any Court, Judge, Magistrate, British Consul or Vice Consul, or representative of Her Majesty or of the Government of India, was so executed and authenticated.

Presumption as to certified copies of foreign judicial records.

86. The Court may presume that any document purporting to be a certified copy of any judicial record of any country not forming part of Her Majesty's dominions is genuine and accurate, if the document purports to be certified in any manner which is certified by any representative of Her Majesty

or of the Government of India resident in such country to be the manner commonly in use in that country for the certification of copies of judicial records.

Presumption as to books, maps, and charts.

87. The Court may presume that any book to which it may refer for information on matters of public or general interest, and that any published map or chart, the statements of which are relevant facts, and which is produced for its inspection, was written and published by the person, and at the time and place, by whom or at which it purports to have been written or published.

Presumption as to telegraph messages.

88. The Court may presume that a message, forwarded from a telegraph office to the person to whom such message purports to be addressed, corresponds with a message delivered for transmission at the office from which the message purports to be sent; but the Court shall not make any presumption as to the person by whom such message was delivered for transmission.

Presumption as to due execution, &c., of documents not produced.

89. The Court shall presume that every document, called for and not produced after notice to produce, was attested, stamped and executed in the manner required by law.

Presumption as to documents thirty years old.

90. Where any document, purporting or proved to be thirty years old, is produced from any custody which the Court in the particular case considers proper, the Court may presume that the signature and every other part of such document, which purports to be in the handwriting of any particular person, is in that person's handwriting, and, in the case of a document executed or attested, that it was duly executed and attested by the persons by whom it purports to be executed and attested.

Explanation.—Documents are said to be in proper custody if they are in the place in which, and under the care of the person with whom they would naturally be; but no custody is improper if it is proved to have had a legitimate origin, or if the circumstances of the particular case are such as to render such an origin probable.

This explanation applies also to section eighty-one.

Illustrations.

(*a.*) A has been in possession of landed property for a long time. He produces from his custody deeds relating to the land showing his title to it. The custody is proper.

(*b.*) A produces deeds relating to landed property of which he is the mortgagee. The mortgagor is in possession. The custody is proper.

(*c.*) A, a connection of B, produces deeds relating to lands in B's possession, which were deposited with him by B for safe custody. The custody is proper.

Chapter VI.—Of the Exclusion of Oral by Documentary Evidence.

Evidence of terms of contracts, grants and other dispositions of property reduced to form of document.

91. When the terms of a contract, or of a grant, or of any other disposition of property, have been reduced to the form of a document, and in all cases in which any matter is required by law to be reduced to the form of a document, no evidence shall be given in proof of the terms of such contract, grant or other disposition of property, or of such matter, except the document itself, or secondary evidence of its contents in cases in which secondary evidence is admissible under the provisions hereinbefore contained.

Exception 1.—When a public officer is required by law to be appointed in writing, and when it is shown that any particular person has acted as such officer, the writing by which he is appointed need not be proved.

Exception 2.—Wills ~~under the Indian Succession Act~~ admitted to probate in British India may be proved by the probate.

Explanation 1.—This section applies equally to cases in which the contracts, grants or dispositions of property referred to are contained in one document, and to cases in which they are contained in more documents than one.

Explanation 2.—Where there are more originals than one, one original only need be proved.

Explanation 3.—The statement, in any document whatever, of a fact other than the facts referred to in this section, shall not preclude the admission of oral evidence as to the same fact.

Illustrations.

(*a.*) If a contract be contained in several letters, all the letters in which it is contained must be proved.

(*b.*) If a contract is contained in a bill of exchange, the bill of exchange must be proved.

(*c.*) If a bill of exchange is drawn in a set of three, one only need be proved.

(*d.*) A contracts, in writing, with B, for the delivery of indigo upon certain terms. The contract mentions the fact that B had paid A the price of other indigo contracted for verbally on another occasion.

Oral evidence is offered that no payment was made for the other indigo. The evidence is admissible.

(*e.*) A gives B a receipt for money paid by B.

Oral evidence is offered of the payment.

The evidence is admissible.

Exclusion of evidence of oral agreement.

92. When the terms of any such contract, grant or other disposition of property, or any matter required by law to be reduced to the form of a document, have been proved according to the last section, no evidence of any oral agreement or statement shall be admitted, as between the parties to any such instrument or their representatives in interest, for the purpose of contradicting, varying, adding to, or subtracting from, its terms:

Proviso. (1.)—Any fact may be proved which would invalidate any document, or which would entitle any person to any decree or order relating thereto; such as fraud, intimidation, illegality, want of due execution, want of capacity in any contracting party, want of failure of consideration, or mistake in fact or law.

Proviso (2.)—The existence of any separate oral agreement as to any matter on which a document is silent, and which is not inconsistent with its terms, may be proved. In considering whether or not this proviso applies, the Court shall have regard to the degree of formality of the document.

Proviso (3.)—The existence of any separate oral agreement, constituting a condition precedent to the attaching of any obligation under any such contract, grant or disposition of property, may be proved.

Proviso (4.)—The existence of any distinct subsequent oral agreement to rescind or modify any such contract, grant or disposition of property, may be proved, except in cases in which such contract, grant or disposition of property is by law required to be in writing, or has been registered according to the law in force for the time being as to the registration of documents.

Proviso (5.)—Any usage or custom by which incidents not expressly mentioned in any contract are usually annexed to contracts of that description, may be proved: Provided that the annexing of such incident would not be repugnant to, or inconsistent with, the express terms of the contract.

Proviso (6.)—Any fact may be proved which shows in what manner the language of a document is related to existing facts.

Illustrations.

(*a.*) A policy of insurance is effected on goods 'in ships from Calcutta to London.' The goods are shipped in a particular ship which is lost. The fact that that particular ship was orally excepted from the policy, cannot be proved.

(*b.*) A agrees absolutely in writing, to pay B Rs. 1,000 on the first of March, 1873. The fact that, at the same time, an oral agreement was made that the money should not be paid till the thirty-first March, cannot be proved.

(*c.*) An estate called 'the Rampur tea estate' is sold by a deed which contains a map of the property sold. The fact that land not included in the map had always been regarded as part of the estate and was meant to pass by the deed, cannot be proved.

(*d.*) A enters into a written contract with B to work certain mines, the property of B, upon certain terms. A was induced to do so by a misrepresentation of B as to their value. This fact may be proved.

(*e.*) A institutes a suit against B for the specific performance of a contract, and also prays that the contract may be reformed as to one of its provisions, as that provision was inserted in it by mistake. A may prove that such a mistake was made as would by law entitle him to have the contract reformed.

(*f.*) A orders goods of B by a letter in which nothing is said as to the time of payment, and accepts the goods on delivery. B sues A for the price. A may show that the goods were supplied on credit for a term still unexpired.

(*g.*) A sells B a horse and verbally warrants him sound. A gives B a paper in these words: 'Bought of A a horse for Rs. 500.' B may prove the verbal warranty.

(*h.*) A hires lodgings of B, and gives B a card on which is written —'Rooms, Rs. 200 a month.' A may prove a verbal agreement that these terms were to include partial board.

A hires lodgings of B for a year, and a regularly stamped agreement, drawn up by an attorney, is made between them. It is silent on the subject of board. A may not prove that board was included in the terms verbally.

(*i.*) A applies to B for a debt due to A by sending a receipt for the money. B keeps the receipt and does not send the money. In a suit for the amount A may prove this.

(*j.*) A and B make a contract in writing to take effect upon the happening of a certain contingency. The writing is left with B who sues A upon it. A may show the circumstances under which it was delivered.

Exclusion of evidence to explain or amend ambiguous document.

93. When the language used in a document is, on its face, ambiguous or defective, evidence may not be given of facts which would show its meaning or supply its defects.

Illustrations.

(*a.*) A agrees, in writing, to sell a horse to B for 'Rs. 1000, or Rs. 1,500.'

Evidence cannot be given to show which price was to be given.

(*b.*) A deed contains blanks. Evidence cannot be given of facts which would show how they were meant to be filled.

Exclusion of evidence against application of document to existing facts.

94. When language used in a document is plain in itself, and when it applies accurately to existing facts, evidence may not be given to show that it was not meant to apply to such facts.

Illustration.

A sells to B, by deed, 'my estate at Rampur containing 100 bighas.' A has an estate at Rampur containing 100 bighas. Evidence may not be given of the fact that the estate meant to be sold was one situated at a different place and of a different size.

Evidence as to document unmeaning in reference to existing facts.

95. When language used in a document is plain in itself, but is unmeaning in reference to existing facts, evidence may be given to show that it was used in a peculiar sense.

Illustration.

A sells to B, by deed, 'my house in Calcutta.'

A had no house in Calcutta, but it appears that he had a house at Howrah, of which B had been in possession since the execution of the deed.

These facts may be proved to show that the deed related to the house at Howrah.

Evidence as to application of language which can apply to one only of several persons or things.

96. When the facts are such that the language used might have been meant to apply to any one, and could not have been meant to apply to more than one, of several persons or things, evidence may be given of facts which show which of those persons or things it was intended to apply to.

Illustrations.

(*a.*) A agrees to sell to B, for Rs. 1,000, 'my white horse.' A has two white horses. Evidence may be given of facts which show which of them was meant.

(*b.*) A agrees to accompany B to Haidarabad. Evidence may be given of facts showing whether Haidarabad in the Dekkhan or Haidarabad in Sindh was meant.

Evidence as to application of language to one of two sets of facts, to neither of which the whole correctly applies.

97. When the language used applies partly to one set of existing facts, and partly to another set of existing facts, but the whole of it does not apply correctly to either, evidence may be given to show to which of the two it was meant to apply.

Illustration.

A agrees to sell to B 'my land at X in the occupation of Y.' A has land at X, but not in the occupation of Y, and he has land in the occupation of Y, but it is not at X. Evidence may be given of facts showing which he meant to sell.

Evidence as to meaning of illegible characters, &c.

98. Evidence may be given to show the meaning of illegible or not commonly intelligible characters, of foreign, obsolete, technical, local, and provincial expressions, of abbreviations and of words used in a peculiar sense.

Illustration.

A, a sculptor, agrees to sell to B 'all my mods.' A has both models and modelling tools. Evidence may be given to show which he meant to sell.

99. Persons who are not parties to a document, or their representatives in interest, may give evidence of any facts tending to show a contemporaneous agreement varying the terms of the document.

Who may give evidence of agreement varying terms of document.

Illustration.

A and B make a contract in writing that B shall sell A certain cotton, to be paid for on delivery. At the same time they make an oral agreement that three months' credit shall be given to A. This could not be shown as between A and B, but it might be shown by C, if it affected his interests.

100. Nothing in this chapter contained shall be taken to affect any of the provisions of the Indian Succession Act (X. of 1865) as to the construction of wills.

Saving of provisions of Indian Succession Act relating to wills.

PART III.

PRODUCTION AND EFFECT OF EVIDENCE.

CHAPTER VII.—OF THE BURDEN OF PROOF.

Burden of proof.

101. Whoever desires any Court to give judgment as to any legal right or liability dependent on the existence of facts which he asserts, must prove that those facts exist.

When a person is bound to prove the existence of any fact, it is said that the burden of proof lies on that person.

Illustrations.

(*a*.) A desires a Court to give judgment that B shall be punished for a crime which A says B has committed.

A must prove that B has committed the crime.

(*b*) A desires a Court to give judgment that he is entitled to certain land in the possession of B, by reason of facts which he asserts, and which B denies, to be true.

A must prove the existence of those facts.

On whom burden of proof lies.

102. The burden of proof in a suit or proceeding lies on that person who would fail if no evidence at all were given on either side.

Illustrations.

(*a*.) A sues B for land of which B is in possession, and which, as A asserts, was left to A by the will of C, B's father.

If no evidence were given on either side, B would be entitled to retain his possession.

Therefore the burden of proof is on A.

(*b*.) A sues B for money due on a bond.

The execution of the bond is admitted, but B says that it was obtained by fraud, which A denies.

If no evidence were given on either side, A would succeed, as the bond is not disputed and the fraud is not proved.

Therefore the burden of proof is on B.

103. The burden of proof as to any particular fact lies on that person who wishes the Court to believe in its existence, unless it is provided by any law that the proof of that fact shall lie on any particular person. Burden of proof as to particular fact.

Illustration.

(*a.*) A prosecutes B for theft, and wishes the Court to believe that B admitted the theft to C. A must prove the admission.

B wishes the Court to believe that, at the time in question, he was elsewhere. He must prove it.

104. The burden of proving any fact necessary to be proved in order to enable any person to give evidence of any other fact is on the person who wishes to give such evidence. Burden of proving fact to be proved to make evidence admissible.

Illustrations.

(*a.*) A wishes to prove a dying declaration by B. A must prove B's death.

(*b.*) A wishes to prove, by secondary evidence, the contents of a lost document.

A must prove that the document has been lost.

105. When a person is accused of any offence, the burden of proving the existence of circumstances bringing the case within any of the General Exceptions in the Indian Penal Code, or within any special exception or proviso contained in any other part of the same Code, or in any law defining the offence, is upon him, and the Court shall presume the absence of such circumstances. Burden of proving that case of accused comes within exceptions.

Illustrations.

(*a.*) A, accused of murder, alleges that, by reason of unsoundness of mind, he did not know the nature of the act.

The burden of proof is on A.

(*b.*) A, accused of murder, alleges that, by grave and sudden provocation, he was deprived of the power of self-control.

The burden of proof is on A.

(*c.*) Section three hundred and twenty-five of the Indian Penal Code provides, that whoever, except in the case provided for by section three hundred and thirty-five, voluntarily causes grievous hurt, shall be subject to certain punishments.

A is charged with voluntarily causing grievous hurt under section three hundred and twenty-five.

The burden of proving the circumstances, bringing the case under section three hundred and thirty-five, lies on A.

Burden of proving fact especially within knowledge.

106. When any fact is especially within the knowledge of any person, the burden of proving that fact is upon him.

Illustrations.

(*a.*) When a person does an act with some intention other than that which the character and circumstances of the act suggest, the burden of proving that intention is upon him.

(*b.*) A is charged with travelling on a railway without a ticket. The burden of proving that he had a ticket is on him.

Burden of proving death of person known to have been alive within thirty years.

107. When the question is whether a man is alive or dead, and it is shown that he was alive within thirty years, the burden of proving that he is dead is on the person who affirms it.

Burden of proving that person is alive who has not been heard of for seven years.

108. When the question is whether a man is alive or dead, and it is proved that he has not been heard of for seven years by those who would naturally have heard of him if he had been alive, the burden of proving that he is alive is on the person who affirms it.

Burden of proof as to relationship in the cases of partners, landlord and tenant, principal and agent.

109. When the question is whether persons are partners, landlord and tenant, or principal and agent, and it has been shown that they have been acting as such, the burden of proving that they do not stand, or have ceased to stand, to each other in those relationships respectively, is on the person who affirms it.

Burden of proof as to ownership.

110. When the question is whether any person is owner of anything of which he is shown to be in possession, the burden of proving that he is not the owner is on the person who affirms that he is not the owner.

Proof of good faith in transactions where one party is in relation of active confidence.

111. Where there is a question as to the good faith of a transaction between parties, one of whom stands to the other in a position of active confidence, the burden of proving the good faith of the transaction is on the party who is in a position of active confidence.

Illustrations.

(*a.*) The good faith of a sale by a client to an attorney is in question in a suit brought by a client. The burden of proving the good faith of the transaction is on the attorney.

(*b.*) The good faith of a sale by a son just come of age to a father is in question in a suit brought by the son. The burden of proving the good faith of the transaction is on the father.

112. The fact that any person was born during the continuance of a valid marriage between his mother and any man, or within two hundred and eighty days after its dissolution, the mother remaining unmarried, shall be conclusive proof that he is the legitimate son of that man, unless it can be shown that the parties had no access to each other at any time when he could have been begotten.

Birth during marriage conclusive proof of legitimacy.

113. A notification in the *Gazette of India* that any portion of British territory has been ceded to any Native State, Prince or Ruler, shall be conclusive proof that a valid cession of such territory took place at the date mentioned in such notification.

Proof of cession of territory.

114. The Court may presume the existence of any fact which it thinks likely to have happened, regard being had to the common course of natural events, human conduct and public and private business in their relation to the facts of the particular case.

Court may presume existence of certain facts.

Illustrations.

The Court may presume—

(*a.*) That a man who is in possession of stolen goods soon after the theft is either the thief, or has received the goods knowing them to be stolen, unless he can account for his possession;

(*b.*) That an accomplice is unworthy of credit, unless he is corroborated in material particulars;

(*c.*) That a bill of exchange, accepted or endorsed, was accepted or endorsed for good consideration;

(*d.*) That a thing or state of things which has been shown to be in existence within a period shorter than that within which such things or states of things usually cease to exist, is still in existence;

(*e.*) That judicial and official acts have been regularly performed;

(*f.*) That the common course of business has been followed in particular cases;

(*g.*) That evidence which could be and is not produced would, if produced, be unfavourable to the person who withholds it;

(*h.*) That if a man refuses to answer a question which he is not compelled to answer by law, the answer, if given, would be unfavourable to him;

(*i.*) That when a document creating an obligation is in the hands of the obligor, the obligation has been discharged.

But the Court shall also have regard to such facts as the following, in considering whether such maxims do or do not apply to the particular case before it:

As to illustration (*a*)—A shop-keeper has in his till a marked rupee soon after it was stolen, and cannot account for its possession specifically, but is continually receiving rupees in the course of his business:

As to illustration (*b*)—A, a person of the highest character, is tried for causing a man's death by an act of negligence in arranging certain machinery. B, a person of equally good character, who also took part in the arrangement, describes precisely what was done, and admits and explains the common carelessness of A and himself:

As to illustration (*b*)—A crime is committed by several persons. A, B and C, three of the criminals, are captured on the spot and kept apart from each other. Each gives an account of the crime implicating D, and the accounts corroborate each other in such a manner as to render previous concert highly improbable:

As to illustration (*c*)—A, the drawer of a bill of exchange, was a man of business. B, the acceptor, was a young and ignorant person, completely under A's influence:

As to illustration (*d*)—It is proved that a river ran in a certain course five years ago, but it is known that there have been floods since that time which might change its course:

As to illustration (*e*)—A judicial act, the regularity of which is in question, was performed under exceptional circumstances:

As to illustration (*f*)—The question is, whether a letter was received. It is shown to have been posted, but the usual course of the post was interrupted by disturbances:

As to illustration (*g*)—A man refuses to produce a document which would bear on a contract of small importance on which he is sued, but which might also injure the feelings and reputation of his family:

As to illustration (*h*)—A man refuses to answer a question which he is not compelled by law to answer, but the answer to it might cause loss to him in matters unconnected with the matters in relation to which he is asked:

As to illustration (*i*)—A bond is in possession of the obligor, but the circumstances of the case are such that he may have stolen it.

CHAPTER VIII.—ESTOPPEL.

115. When one person has, by his declaration, act or omission, intentionally caused or permitted another person to believe a thing to be true and to act upon such a belief, neither he nor his representative shall be allowed, in any suit or proceeding between himself and such person or his representative, to deny the truth of that thing. Estoppel.

Illustration.

A intentionally and falsely leads B to believe that certain land belongs to A, and thereby induces B to buy and pay for it.

The land afterwards becomes the property of A, and A seeks to set aside the sale on the ground that, at the time of the sale, he had no title. He must not be allowed to prove his want of title.

116. No tenant of immoveable property, or person claiming through such tenant, shall, during the continuance of the tenancy, be permitted to deny that the landlord of such tenant had, at the beginning of the tenancy, a title to such immoveable property; and no person who came upon any immoveable property by the license of the person in the possession thereof, shall be permitted to deny that such person had a title to such possession at the time when such license was given. Estoppel of tenant; and of licensee of person in possession.

117. No acceptor of a bill of exchange shall be permitted to deny that the drawer had authority to draw such bill or to endorse it; nor shall any bailee or licensee be permitted to deny that his bailor or licensor had, at the time when the bailment or license commenced, authority to make such bail ment or grant such license. Estoppel of acceptor of bill of exchange, bailee, or licensee.

Explanation (1.)—The acceptor of a bill of exchange may deny that the bill was really drawn by the person by whom it purports to have been drawn.

Explanation (2.)—If a bailee delivers the goods bailed to a person other than the bailor, he may prove that such person had a right to them as against the bailor.

CHAPTER IX.—OF WITNESSES.

Who may testify.

118. All persons shall be competent to testify unless t Court considers that they are prevented from understandi the questions put to them, or from giving rational answers those questions, by tender years, extreme old age, diseas whether of body or mind, or any other cause of the san kind.

Explanation.—A lunatic is not incompetent to testif unless he is prevented by his lunacy from understanding th questions put to him and giving rational answers to them.

Dumb witnesses.

119. A witness who is unable to speak may give his ev dence in any other manner in which he can make it inte ligible, as by writing or by signs; but such writing must b written and the signs made in open Court. Evidence s given shall be deemed to be oral evidence.

Parties to civil suit, and their wives or husbands. Husband or wife of person under criminal trial.

120. In all civil proceedings the parties to the suit, an the husband or wife of any party to the suit, shall be com petent witnesses. In criminal proceedings against any pe son, the husband or wife of such person, respectively, sha be a competent witness.

Judges and Magistrates.

121. No Judge or Magistrate shall, except upon the specia order of some Court to which he is subordinate, be compelle to answer any questions as to his own conduct in Court a such Judge or Magistrate, or as to anything which came t his knowledge in Court as such Judge or Magistrate; but h may be examined as to other matters which occurred in hi presence while he was so acting.

Illustrations.

(*a.*) A, on his trial before the Court of Session, says that a depo sition was improperly taken by B, the Magistrate. B cannot b compelled to answer questions as to this, except upon the specia order of a superior Court.

(*b.*) A is accused before the Court of Session of having given fals evidence before B, a Magistrate. B cannot be asked what A said except upon the special order of the superior Court.

(*c.*) A is accused before the Court of Session of attempting t murder a Police officer whilst on his trial before B, a Sessions Judge. B may be examined as to what occurred.

Communications during marriage.

122. No person who is or has been married, shall be compelled to disclose any communication made to him during marriage by any person to whom he is or has been married; nor shall he be permitted to disclose any such communication, unless the person who made it, or his representative in interest, consents, except in suits between married persons, or proceedings in which one married person is prosecuted for any crime committed against the other.

Evidence as to affairs of State.

123. No one shall be permitted to give any evidence derived from unpublished official records relating to any affairs of State, except with the permission of the officer at the head of the department concerned, who shall give or withhold such permission as he thinks fit.

Official communications.

124. No public officer shall be compelled to disclose communications made to him in official confidence, when he considers that the public interests would suffer by the disclosure.

Information as to commission of offences.

125. No Magistrate or Police officer shall be compelled to say whence he got any information as to the commission of any offence.

Professional communication.

126. No barrister, attorney, pleader or vakíl, shall at any time be permitted, unless with his client's express consent, to disclose any communication made to him in the course and for the purpose of his employment as such barrister, pleader, attorney or vakíl, by or on behalf of his client, or to state the contents or condition of any document with which he has become acquainted in the course and for the purpose of his professional employment, or to disclose any advice given by him to his client in the course and for the purpose of such employment:

Provided that nothing in this section shall protect from disclosure—

(1.) Any such communication made in furtherance of any criminal purpose;

(2.) Any fact observed by any barrister, pleader, attorney,

or vakíl, in the course of his employment as such, showing that any crime or fraud has been committed since the commencement of his employment.

It is immaterial whether the attention of such barrister, attorney or vakíl was or was not directed to such fact by or on behalf of his client.

Explanation.—The obligation stated in this section continnes after the employment has ceased.

Illustrations.

(*a.*) A, a client, says to B, an attorney—'I have committed forgery, and I wish you to defend me.'

As the defence of a man known to be guilty is not a criminal purpose, this communication is protected from disclosure.

(*b.*) A, a client, says to B, an attorney—'I wish to obtain possession of property by the use of a forged deed on which I request you to sue.'

This communication, being made in furtherance of a criminal purpose, is not protected from disclosure.

(*c.*) A, being charged with embezzlement, retains B, an attorney, to defend him. In the course of the proceedings, B observes that an entry has been made in A's account-book, charging A with the sum said to have been embezzled, which entry was not in the book, at the commencement of his employment.

This being a fact observed by B in the course of his employment showing that a fraud has been committed since the commencement of the proceedings, it is not protected from disclosure.

Section 126 to apply to interpreters, &c.

127. The provisions of section one hundred and twenty-six shall apply to interpreters, and the clerks or servants of barristers, pleaders, attorneys and vakíls.

Privilege not waived by volunteering evidence.

128. If any party to a suit gives evidence therein at his own instance or otherwise, he shall not be deemed to have consented thereby to such disclosure as is mentioned in section one hundred and twenty-six; and if any party to a suit or proceeding calls any such barrister, attorney, or vakíl as a witness, he shall be deemed to have consented to such disclosure only if he questions such barrister, attorney or vakíl on matters which, but for such question, he would not be at liberty to disclose.

129. No one shall be compelled to disclose to the Court any confidential communication which has taken place between him and his legal professional adviser, unless he offers himself as a witness, in which case he may be compelled to disclose any such communications as may appear to the Court necessary to be known in order to explain any evidence which he has given, but no others.

Confidential communications with legal advisers.

130. No witness who is not a party to a suit shall be compelled to produce his title-deeds to any property, or any document in virtue of which he holds any property as pledgee or mortgagee, or any document the production of which might tend to criminate him, unless he has agreed in writing to produce them with the person seeking the production of such deeds or some person through whom he claims.

Production of title-deeds of witness not a party.

131. No one shall be compelled to produce documents in his possession which any other person would be entitled to refuse to produce if they were in his possession, unless such last mentioned person consents to their production.

Production of documents which another person, having possession, could refuse to produce.

132. A witness shall not be excused from answering any question as to any matter relevant to the matter in issue in any suit or in any civil or criminal proceeding, upon the ground that the answer to such question will criminate, or may tend directly or indirectly to criminate, such witness, or that it will expose, or tend directly or indirectly to expose, such witness to a penalty or forfeiture of any kind:

Witness not excused from answering on ground that answer will criminate.

Provided that no such answer, which a witness shall be compelled to give, shall subject him to any arrest or prosecution, or be proved against him in any criminal proceeding, except a prosecution for giving false evidence by such answer.

Proviso.

133. An accomplice shall be a competent witness against an accused person; and a conviction is not illegal merely because it proceeds upon the uncorroborated testimony of an accomplice.

Accomplice.

134. No particular number of witnesses shall in any case be required for the proof of any fact.

Number of witnesses.

CHAPTER X.—OF THE EXAMINATION OF WITNESSES.

Order of production and examination of witnesses.

135. The order in which witnesses are produced and examined shall be regulated by the law and practice for the time being relating to civil and criminal procedure respectively, and, in the absence of any such law, by the discretion of the Court.

Judge to decide as to admissibility of evidence.

136. When either party proposes to give evidence of any fact, the Judge may ask the party proposing to give the evidence in what manner the alleged fact, if proved, would be relevant; and the Judge shall admit the evidence if he thinks that the fact, if proved, would be relevant, and not otherwise.

If the fact proposed to be proved is one of which evidence is admissible only upon proof of some other fact, such last-mentioned fact must be proved before evidence is given of the fact first mentioned, unless the party undertakes to give proof of such fact, and the Court is satisfied with such undertaking.

If the relevancy of one alleged fact depends upon another alleged fact being first proved, the Judge may, in his discretion, either permit evidence of the first fact to be given before the second fact is proved, or require evidence to be given of the second fact before evidence is given of the first fact.

Illustrations.

(*a*.) It is proposed to prove a statement about a relevant fact by a person alleged to be dead, which statement is relevant under section thirty-two.

The fact that the person is dead must be proved by the person proposing to prove the statement, before evidence is given of the statement.

(*b*.) It is proposed to prove, by a copy, the contents of a document said to be lost.

The fact that the original is lost must be proved by the person proposing to produce the copy, before the copy is produced.

(*c*.) A is accused of receiving stolen property knowing it to have been stolen.

It is proposed to prove that he denied the possession of the property.

The relevancy of the denial depends on the identity of the property. The Court may in its discretion, either require the property to be identified before the denial of the possession is proved, or permit the denial of the possession to be proved before the property is identified.

(*d.*) It is proposed to prove a fact (A) which is said to have been the cause or effect of a fact in issue. There are several intermediate facts (B, C and D) which must be shown to exist before the fact (A) can be regarded as the cause or effect of the fact in issue. The Court may either permit A to be proved before B, C or D is proved, or may require proof of B, C and D before permitting proof of A.

137. The examination of a witness by the party who calls him shall be called his examination-in-chief. *Examination-in-chief.*

The examination of a witness by the adverse party shall be called his cross-examination. *Cross-examination.*

The examination of a witness, subsequent to the cross-examination by the party who called him, shall be called his re-examination. *Re-examination.*

138. Witnesses shall be first examined-in-chief, then (if the adverse party so desires) cross-examined, then (if the party so desires) be re-examined. *Order of examinations.*

The examination and cross-examination must relate to relevant facts, but the cross-examination need not be confined to the facts to which the witness testified on his examination-in-chief.

The re-examination shall be directed to the explanation of matters referred to in cross-examination; and if new matter is, by permission of the Court, introduced in re-examination, the adverse party may further cross-examine upon that matter. *Direction of re-examination.*

139. A person summoned to produce a document does not become a witness by the mere fact that he produced it, and cannot be cross-examined unless and until he is called as a witness. *Cross-examination of person called to produce a document.*

140. Witnesses to character may be cross-examined and re-examined. *Witnesses to character.*

Leading questions.

141. Any question suggesting the answer which the person putting it wishes or expects to receive, is called a leading question.

When they must not be asked.

142. Leading questions must not, if objected to by the adverse party, be asked in an examination-in-chief, or in a re-examination, except with the permission of the Court.

The Court shall permit leading questions as to matters which are introductory or undisputed, or which have, in its opinion, been already sufficiently proved.

When they may be asked.

143. Leading questions may be asked in cross-examination.

Evidence as to matters in writing.

144. Any witness may be asked, whilst under examination, whether any contract, grant or other disposition of property. as to which he is giving evidence, was not contained in a document, and if he says that it was, or if he is about to make any statement as to the contents of any document, which, in the opinion of the Court, ought to be produced, the adverse party may object to such evidence being given until such document is produced, or until facts have been proved which entitle the party who called the witness to give secondary evidence of it.

Explanation.—A witness may give oral evidence of state ments made by other persons about the contents of documents if such statements are in themselves relevant facts.

Illustration.

The question is, whether A assaulted B.

C deposes that he heard A say to D— 'B wrote a letter accusing me of theft, and I will be revenged on him.' This statement is relevant, as showing A's motive for the assault, and evidence may be given of it, though no other evidence is given about the letter.

Cross-examination as to previous statements in writing.

145. A witness may be cross-examined as to previous statements made by him in writing, or reduced into writing, and relevant to matters in question, without such writing being shown to him, or being proved; but if it is intended to contradict him by the writing, his intention must, before

the writing can be proved, be called to those parts of it which are to be used for the purpose of contradicting him.

Questions lawful in cross-examination.

146. When a witness is cross-examined, he may, in addition to the questions hereinbefore referred to, be asked any questions which tend

(1) to test his veracity;

(2) to discover who he is, and what is his position in life; or

(3) to shake his credit, by injuring his character, although the answer to such questions might tend directly or indirectly to criminate him, or might expose or tend directly or indirectly to expose him to a penalty or forfeiture.

When witness to be compelled to answer.

147. If any such question relates to a matter relevant to the suit or proceeding, the provisions of section one hundred and thirty-two shall apply thereto.

Court to decide when question shall be asked and when witness compelled to answer.

148. If any such question relates to a matter not relevant to the suit or proceeding, except in so far as it affects the credit of the witness by injuring his character, the Court shall decide whether or not the witness shall be compelled to answer it, and may, if it thinks fit, warn the witness that he is not obliged to answer it. In exercising its discretion, the Court shall have regard to the following considerations:—

(1.) Such questions are proper if they are of such a nature that the truth of the imputation conveyed by them would seriously affect the opinion of the Court as to the credibility of the witness on the matter to which he testifies;

(2.) Such questions are improper if the imputation which they convey relates to matters so remote in time, or of such a character, that the truth of the imputation would not affect, or would affect in a slight degree, the opinion of the Court as to the credibility of the witness on the matter to which he testifies;

(3.) Such questions are improper if there is a great disproportion between the importance of the imputation made against the witness's character and the importance of his evidence;

(4.) The Court may, if it sees fit, draw, from the witness's refusal to answer, the inference that the answer if given would be unfavourable.

Question not to be asked without reasonable grounds.

149. No such question as is referred to in section one hundred and forty-eight ought to be asked, unless the person asking it has reasonable grounds for thinking that the imputation which it conveys is well-founded.

Illustrations.

(*a.*) A barrister is instructed by an attorney or vakíl that an important witness is a dakait. This is reasonable ground for asking the witness whether he is a dakait.

(*b.*) A pleader is informed by a person in Court that an important witness is a dakait. The informant, on being questioned by the pleader, gives satisfactory reasons for his statement. This is a reasonable ground for asking the witness whether he is a dakait.

(*c.*) A witness, of whom nothing whatever is known, is asked at random whether he is a dakait. There are here no reasonable grounds for the question.

(*d.*) A witness, of whom nothing whatever is known, being questioned as to his mode of life and means of living, gives unsatisfactory answers. This may be a reasonable ground for asking him if he is a dakait.

Procedure of Court in case of question being asked without reasonable grounds.

150. If the Court is of opinion that any such question was asked without reasonable grounds, it may, if it was asked by any barrister, pleader, vakíl or attorney, report the circumstances of the case to the High Court or other authority to which such barrister, pleader, vakíl, or attorney is subject in the exercise of his profession.

Indecent and scandalous questions.

151. The Court may forbid any questions or inquiries which it regards as indecent or scandalous, although such questions or inquiries may have some bearing on the questions before the Court, unless they relate to facts in issue, or to matters necessary to be known in order to determine whether or not the facts in issue existed.

Questions intended to insult or annoy.

152. The Court shall forbid any question which appears to it to be intended to insult or annoy, or which, though proper in itself, appears to the Court needlessly offensive in form.

153. When a witness has been asked and has answered any question which is relevant to the inquiry only in so far as it tends to shake his credit by injuring his character, no evidence shall be given to contradict him; but if he answers falsely, he may afterwards be charged with giving false evidence.

Exclusion of evidence to contradict answers to questions testing veracity.

Exception 1.—If a witness is asked whether he has been previously convicted of any crime and denies it, evidence may be given of his previous conviction.

Exception 2.—If a witness is asked any question tending to impeach his impartiality, and answers it by denying the facts suggested, he may be contradicted.

Illustration.

(*a.*) A claim against an underwriter is resisted on the ground of fraud.

The claimant is asked whether, in a former transaction, he had not made a fraudulent claim. He denies it.

Evidence is offered to show that he did make such a claim.

The evidence is inadmissible.

(*b.*) A witness is asked whether he was not dismissed from a situation for dishonesty. He denies it.

Evidence is offered to show that he was dismissed for dishonesty.

The evidence is not admissible.

(*c.*) A affirms that on a certain day he saw B at Lahore.

A is asked whether he himself was not on that day at Calcutta. He denies it.

Evidence is offered to show that A was on that day at Calcutta.

The evidence is admissible, not as contradicting A on a fact which affects his credit, but as contradicting the alleged fact that B was seen on the day in question in Lahore.

In each of these cases the witness might, if his denial were false, be charged with giving false evidence.

(*d.*) A is asked whether his family has not had a blood feud with the family of B against whom he gives evidence.

He denies it. He may be contradicted on the ground that the question tends to impeach his impartiality.

154. The Court may, in its discretion, permit the person

Questions by party to

his own witness.

who calls a witness to put any questions to him which mig be put in cross-examination by the adverse party.

Impeaching credit of witness.

155. The credit of a witness may be impeached in t following ways by the adverse party, or, with the consent the Court, by the party who calls him :—

(1.) By the evidence of persons who testify that th from their knowledge of the witness, believe him to be u worthy of credit;

(2.) By proof that the witness has been bribed, or h had the offer of a bribe, or has received any other corru inducement to give his evidence;

(3.) By proof of former statements inconsistent with a part of his evidence which is liable to be contradicted;

(4.) When a man is prosecuted for rape or an attempt ravish, it may be shown that the prosecutrix was of general immoral character.

Explanation.—A witness declaring another witness to unworthy of credit may not, upon his examination-in-ch give reasons for his belief, but he may be asked his reasons cross-examination, and the answers which he gives cannot contradicted, though, if they are false, he may afterwards charged with giving false evidence.

Illustrations.

(*a*). A sues B for the price of goods sold and delivered to B.

C says that he delivered the goods to B.

Evidence is offered to show that, on a previous occasion, he s that he had not delivered the goods to B.

The evidence is admissible.

(*b*.) A is indicted for the murder of B.

C says that B, when dying, declared that A had given B the wou of which he died.

Evidence is offered to show that on a previous occasion, C sa that the wound was not given by A or in his presence.

The evidence is admissible.

Questions tending to corroborate

156. When a witness whom it is intended to corrobora gives evidence of any relevant fact, he may be questioned

to any other circumstances which he observed at or near to the time or place at which such relevant fact occurred, if the Court is of opinion that such circumstances, if proved, would corroborate the testimony of the witness as to the relevant fact which he testifies.

evidence of relevant fact, admissible.

Illustration.

A, an accomplice, gives an account of a robbery in which he took part. He describes various incidents unconnected with the robbery which occurred on his way to and from the place where it was committed.

Independent evidence of these facts may be given in order to corroborate his evidence as to the robbery itself.

Former statements of witness may be proved to corroborate later testimony as to same fact.

157. In order to corroborate the testimony of a witness, any former statement made by such witness relating to the same fact, at or about the time when the fact took place, or before any authority legally competent to investigate the fact, may be proved.

What matters may be proved in connection with proved statement relevant under section 32 or 33.

158. Whenever any statement, relevant under section thirty-two or thirty-three, is proved, all matters may be proved, either in order to contradict or to corroborate it, or in order to impeach or confirm the credit of the person by whom it was made, which might have been proved if that person had been called as a witness, and had denied upon cross-examination the truth of the matter suggested.

Refreshing memory.

159. A witness may, while under examination, refresh his memory by referring to any writing made by himself at the time of the transaction concerning which he is questioned, or so soon afterwards that the Court considers it likely that the transaction was at that time fresh in his memory.

The witness may also refer to any such writing made by any other person, and read by the witness within the time aforesaid, if when he read it he knew it to be correct.

When witness may use copy of document to refresh memory.

Whenever a witness may refresh his memory by reference to any document, he may, with the permission of the Court, refer to a copy of such document, provided the Court be satisfied that there is sufficient reason for the non-production of the original.

An expert may refresh his memory by reference to professional treatises.

Testimony to facts stated in document mentioned in section 159.

160. A witness may also testify to facts mentioned in any such document as is mentioned in section one hundred and fifty-nine, although he has no specific recollection of the facts themselves, if he is sure that the facts were correctly recorded in the document.

Illustration.

A book-keeper may testify to facts recorded by him in books regularly kept in the course of business, if he knows that the books were correctly kept, although he has forgotten the particular transactions entered.

Right of adverse party as to writing used to refresh memory.

161. Any writing referred to under the provisions of the two last preceding sections must be produced and shown to the adverse party if he requires it; such party may, if he pleases, cross-examine the witness thereupon.

Production of documents.

162. A witness summoned to produce a document shall, if it is in his possession or power, bring it to Court, notwithstanding any objection which there may be to its production or to its admissibility. The validity of any such objection shall be decided on by the Court.

The Court, if it sees fit, may inspect the document, unless it refers to matters of State, or take other evidence to enable it to determine on its admissibility.

Translation of documents.

If for such a purpose it is necessary to cause any document to be translated, the Court may, if it thinks fit, direct the translator to keep the contents secret, unless the document is to be given in evidence: and if the interpreter disobeys such direction, he shall be held to have committed an offence under section one hundred and sixty-six of the Indian Penal Code.

Giving, as evidence, of document called for

163. When a party calls for a document which he has given the other party notice to produce, and such document is produced and inspected by the party calling for its pro-

duction, he is bound to give it as evidence if the party producing it requires him to do so.

and produced on notice.

Using, as evidence, of document production of which was refused on notice.

164. When a party refuses to produce a document which he has had notice to produce, he cannot afterwards use the document as evidence without the consent of the other party or the order of the Court.

Illustration.

A sues B on an agreement and gives B notice to produce it. At the trial, A calls for the document and B refuses to produce it. A gives secondary evidence of its contents. B seeks to produce the document itself to contradict the secondary evidence given by A, or in order to show that the agreement is not stamped. He cannot do so.

Judge's power to put questions or order production.

165. The Judge may, in order to discover or to obtain proper proof of relevant facts, ask anv question he pleases, in any form, at any time, of any witness, or of the parties, about any fact, relevant or irrelevant, and may order the production of any document or thing, and neither the parties nor their agents shall be entitled to make any objection to any such question or order, nor, without the leave of the Court, to cross-examine any witness upon any answer given in reply to any such question:

Provided that the judgment must be based upon facts declared by this Act to be relevant, and duly proved:

Provided also that this section shall not authorize any Judge to compel any witness to answer any question, or to produce any document which such witness would be entitled to refuse to answer or produce under sections one hundred and twenty-one to one hundred and thirty-one both inclusive, if the question were asked or the document were called for by the adverse party; nor shall the Judge ask any question which it would be improper for any other person to ask under sections one hundred and forty-eight or one hundred and forty-nine; nor shall he dispense with primary evidence of any document, except in the cases hereinbefore excepted.

Power of jury or

166. In cases tried by jury or with assessors, the jury or

assessors to put questions. assessors may put any questions to the witnesses, through or by leave of the Judge, which the Judge himself might put and which he considers proper.

CHAPTER XI.—OF IMPROPER ADMISSION AND REJECTION OF EVIDENCE.

No new trial for improper admission or rejection of evidence.

167. The improper admission or rejection of evidence shall not be ground of itself for a new trial or reversal of any decision in any case, if it shall appear to the Court before which such objection is raised that, independently of the evidence objected to and admttied, there was sufficient evidence to justify the decision, or that, if the rejected evidence had been received, it ought not to have varied the decision.

SCHEDULE.

ENACTMENTS REPEALED.

[*See section* 2.]

NUMBER AND YEAR	TITLE.	EXTENT OF REPEAL.
Stat. 26 Geo. III. cap. 57.	For the further regulation of the trial of persons accused of certain offences committed in the East Indies; for repealing so much of an Act, made in the twenty-fourth year of the reign of his present Majesty (intituled 'An Act for the better regulation and management of the affairs of the East India Company, and of the British possessions in India, and for establishing a court of judicature for the more speedy and effectual trial of persons accused of offences committed in the East Indies') as requires the servants of the East India Company to deliver inventories of their estates and effects; for rendering the laws more effectual against persons unlawfully resorting to the East Indies; and for the more easy proof, in certain cases, of deeds and writings executed in Great Britain or India.	Section thirty-eight so far as it relates to Courts of justice in the East Indies.
Stat. 14 and 15 Vic., cap. 99.	To amend the Law of Evidence	Section eleven and so much of section nineteen as relates to British India.
Act XV of 1852......	To amend the Law of Evidence	So much as has not been heretofore repealed.
Act XIX of 1853......	To amend the Law of Evidence in the Civil Courts of the East India Company in the Bengal Presidency.	Section nineteen.
Act II of 1855	For the further improvement of the Law of Evidence.	So much as has not been heretofore repealed.
Act XXV of 1861 ...	For simplifying the Procedure of the Courts of Criminal Judicature not established by Royal Charter.	Section two hundred and thirty-seven.
Act I of 1868.........	The General Clauses' Act, 1868	Sections seven and eight.

INDEX TO THE INDIAN EVIDENCE ACT I. OF 1872.

J. AND W. RIDER, PRINTERS, LONDON.

CPSIA information can be obtained at www.ICGtesting.com
Printed in the USA
BVOW06s0833220916

462974BV00018B/105/P

9 781331 42